WITHDRAWN
HARVARD LIBRARY
WITHDRAWN

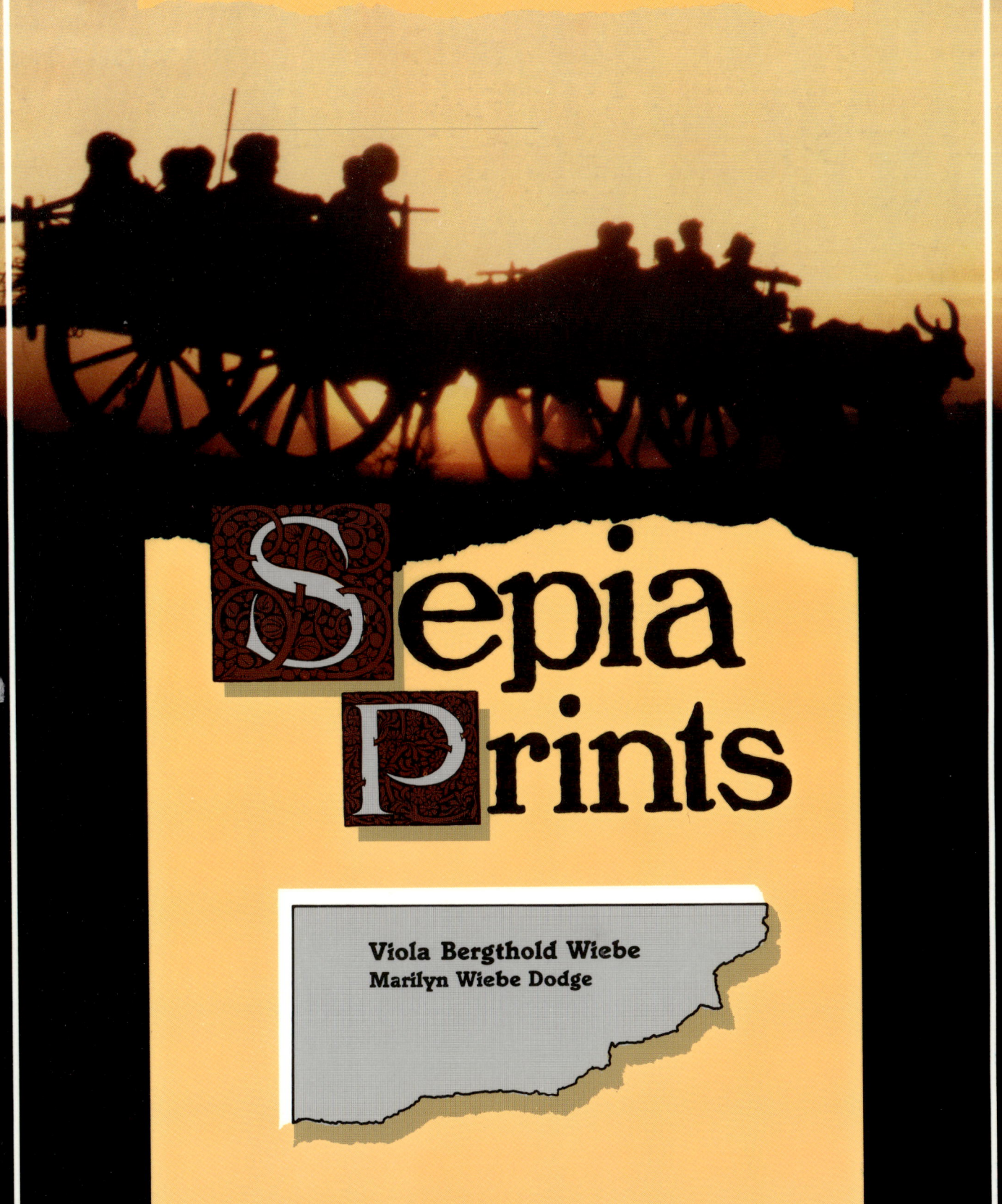

MEMOIRS OF A MISSIONARY IN INDIA

Sepia Prints

Viola Bergthold Wiebe
Marilyn Wiebe Dodge

A SCRAPBOOK

KINDRED PRESS

Sepia Prints

Memoirs of a missionary in India

VIOLA BERGTHOLD WIEBE
Marilyn Wiebe Dodge

Sepia Prints

Viola Bergthold Wiebe
Marilyn Wiebe Dodge

MEMOIRS OF A MISSIONARY IN INDIA

Winnipeg, MB Canada   Kindred Press   Hillsboro, KS USA

SEPIA PRINTS
Memoirs of a Missionary
in India

First Edition

Author — Viola Bergthold Wiebe
CoAuthor — Marilyn Wiebe Dodge

© 1990 Kindred Press
Winnipeg, Manitoba
Canada

All rights reserved. No part of this book may be reproduced or transmitted in any form or by any means without written permission from the publisher, except by a reviewer, who may quote brief passages in a review.

Published simultaneously by

Kindred Press
Hillsboro, KS 67063
U.S.A.

Kindred Press
Winnipeg, MB R2L 2E5
Canada

Design and layout by D. Andrew West and Stan Friesen, Multi Business Press

Printed in the United States by Multi Business Press, Hillsboro, KS

Assistance for the publication of this book has been received from the Center for MB Studies and the Wiebe family.

International Standard Book Number:
0-921788-03-7

"God's will, nothing else, nothing less, nothing more, is my aim"
Daniel F. Bergthold
Jan. 12, 1876 — Oct 25, 1948.

My Father, Daniel F. Bergthold, was born on 12 January 1876 in Pyatigorsk, Stavropol, Southern Russia to Henry and Alvina (Starke) Bergthold who were of Galician descent. The name Bergthold was derived from the German *Berchtholdt* from the warrior title von BerchWald or *Brillian Governore*. Descendants were among the early nobility of Berne, Switzerland. Their Coat of Arms had a red heart on a green mound placed below a three-flowered lily-of-the-valley on a gold shield.

Contents

Father Bergthold v
Acknowledgements xi
Preface xiii
Early Missionaries xvii

Book I: 1903–1921   1

Grandparents Mandtler and Bergthold 2
Mother Katharina 3
Mother and Father in America 5
Map of India 6
Language Study 9
Falaknuma Palace 10
Halisika Stamps, Currency 11
Mother's Death 12
Mother Anna 13
Pioneering Nagarkurnool Mission 14
Dress Codes 15
House Help and Workers 17
Nagarkurnool 18
Touring 24
Travel to Russia, America and Back 27
Ootacamund 28
Coonoor Boarding School 29
Mother Anna's Death 32
Hook Festival and Jaggernaut Wagon Pictures 36
Tiger Story 37
Papa's Early Photographs 38
First Car in Mission 39

Book II: 1921–1936   41

Journey to America 42
Parents Depart for India 44
Courtship 46
Graduation 1925, 1926 47
Letters, Snaps 48
Marriage to John 50

Travel to India	53
New Missionaries	54
Caricatures, Language Mistakes	56
F.A. Janzen's Death by Poisoning	58
Wanaparty	59
Esther's Birth	61
John's Birth	63
Devarakonda	65
Kalvakurty	66
Travel to North India	68
Viola Ruth's Birth	70
Home Cures	71
Sketches	72
Irene's Birth	75
Recollections of Four Oldest Children	76
Travel to America	78

Book III: 1936–1961 — 81

Return to India	81
Mahbubnagar	82
The Bungalow	84
Twins' Birth	88
Untouchables	89
Abraham	92
Ankamma	93
Train Recollections	94
"Mugus"	96
Kodaikanal	98
Mission Conference	100
Marilyn's Birth	101
Mission Press	103
Parents' Retirement	105
Return to America: 1946	106
Minnesota, Kansas	108
Parents Wiebe and Bergthold's Deaths	112
Return to India: 1951	114
John's Diary Travelogue	115
Touring	118
Visitors	119
Kodaikanal Social Life	120
Jadcherla: Legal Proceedings	122

Parvathi	123
Mahbubnagar School, Teachers	124
Letters	126
Money Problems	129
Cyclone	130
Train Crash	131
Lombardis	133
Church Dedication	137
Radio Work	138
Farewell to India	140

Book IV: 1961–1970 — 145

Return to India	146
Ramapatnam	147
A Missionary Colleague	148
Dispensary	150
Venkamma	152
John's Death	154
Short Leave in America, Return to India	156
Snake Charmers	158
Solomon Raju	159
Baby Day	160
"One Day"	162
Farewell Address	166
Farewell to India	167
Epilogue	171

Acknowledgements

Sepia Prints is a glimpse at the last days of the British Raj in India and the first days of Independence through the eyes of a missionary who lived and worked among the Telugus of South Central India during this period. The materials used are primarily from personal recollections and experiences. The illustrations were drawn by family members or taken from family albums.

My parents took me to India with them during the first year of my life. All of our children were born in India. My beloved husband John drowned and was buried there in 1963. My love for my parents and family members and for countless other co-workers and friends in India and elsewhere has surfaced continuously in the preparation of this scrapbook. They, together, after all, have given love and meaning to the journey of my life.

My daughter Marilyn worked with me in putting this scrapbook together. Without her art work, skill and encouragement and the pertinent advice and support of her husband, Cole, it would not have been possible for me to work on this scrapbook with them in Khartoum and Kampala.

The caricatures drawn by son John help spice up the text. My children Esther, Ruth, Irene and David encouraged us with pictures and write-ups. I am grateful to son Paul who wrote the preface to *Sepia Prints*.

The rich heritage of faith, love and integrity has been passed down from our parents and I see it in our children who, with their companions, carry on Godly fear, strength and beauty. As the staff is passed on to yet another generation, we recognize God's goodness and faithfulness and that our commitments have not been in vain.

So ends this part of the story which is, of course, incomplete. I pray that it will be to the glory of God and to the encouragement of other pilgrims on the often hazardous and difficult, but also meaningful and pleasurable road of life.

Preface

The Mennonite missionaries accomplished very much on and out of their mission stations. Whether for better or worse in the later development of the church in the region, the mission stations, with their bungalows and medical, educational and other institutions, served as islands between the background contexts from which the missionaries came and the worlds of the villagers in the region.

Much changed in the round of missionary life over the years. Early missionaries traveled by foot, oxcart, horse, buggy or bicycle. Later missionaries were more and more likely to travel by car. The use of tents during periods of extended touring in the villages gave way to the use of homemade trailers sent ahead with teams of oxen. Road and train services developed. The chance to provide better quality medicines and the ability to understand local patterns of life improved. Ordinary kerosene lanterns were replaced by pressure lanterns. Battery operated loudspeakers, slide shows, tracts and other published materials increasingly came into use. As local churches were established, missionaries found that their work had more and more to do with the encouragement and teaching of the Christians already gathered than with the direct further propagation of the gospel. As hospital, educational and other institutional programs developed, new avenues of ministry and service emerged. As mission work grew into church work, the missionaries more and more commonly found Indian co-workers with whom to carry out their responsibilities.

The career experiences of most of the missionaries followed roughly similar patterns. They included, first, intensive periods of language instruction, then assignment to one or another of the mission stations. "Single lady" missionaries (as they were then called) were usually assigned to educational or medical programs, missionary couples to the more general coordination of the work.

The principle work assignments of the doctors and educators became increasingly well-defined with the development of hospitals and schools. Most of the time most of the missionaries were required to do many things: tour villages, encourage literacy efforts, and develop women's and youth programs; produce architectural plans and direct building projects; administer schools in the villages and on the compounds, encourage preachers and coordinate preacher, field association and other meetings; prepare reports and meet with government officials; teach and direct development projects, encourage wavering church members and raise money. The missionaries corresponded with home church, mission board and other individuals interested in their work in other parts of the world. They helped many converts find jobs and ran hostel programs for school children.

With the variety and amount of work that they did, few missionaries had much trouble with boredom. More problematic was the loneliness many of them experienced in the separation from all that was familiar in their home backgrounds. Periodic committee meetings with co-workers helped. So did the annual missionary conferences at which all missionary families gathered for three or four days of fellowship and recreation. And so, of course, did the annual six-week trip to the hills during the hot season. The beautiful South Indian hill stations of Ootacamund and Kodaikanal were also boarding school settings. Here parents could be together with their school-age children from whom they were separated much of the year, and here missionaries could meet others of their own kind on walks and at teas and other planned get-togethers. Yet the problem remained. It was evidenced in the tremendous interest almost all of the missionaries always had in letters from relatives and friends. It was clear in the nostalgia most expressed in their references to "home" no matter how many years they had spent in India. It was clear in the eagerness most felt when the chance to go on furlough actually approached.

The journey to India until late in the 1950s was almost always by ship and usually required at least a month's time. Regular terms of service were never less than five years and sometimes as long as ten years. The fact of being alone and somehow vulnerable in a strange land was at times brought home in abundant clarity in the sickness and occasionally the death of fellow missionaries or loved ones.

Contests and rivalries aplenty occurred among the missionaries over mission procedures, the best way to build the church, or the location of particular facilities and services, and sometimes the rivalries were intense. Heat and dust affected the missionaries differently. So did the intestinal parasites most of them picked up at one time or another. One missionary occasionally threw coins from his upstairs verandah to poor people gathered below, and once dashed out of his bungalow to slash the skin container in which fermented palm juice (*kallu*) was being transported to a nearby jatra. Other missionaries were deeply disturbed by such behavior.

Differences were often problematic. Older missionaries generally held sway over newcomers, whatever the differences in their talents. The common understanding was that an education in mission work in India "began when you first docked in Bombay." Given the need to learn a new language and adjust to a very different socio-cultural environment, such understandings were reasonable in ways. In others they led to the perpetuation of procedures that might well have been changed more quickly and, at times, the exacerbation of personal rivalries.

On the other hand, unities among the missionaries were very strong indeed, and no one who ever heard them sing together the old German favorite, *Nun Ist Sie Erschienen*, towards the end of an annual missionary fellowship would ever doubt this. The missionaries had come out of similar backgrounds and they faced common problems in their work. Whatever their differences, all of them knew they were "called by the Lord" to missionary service in India.

The Christian community founded through the work of the Mennonite Brethren missionaries and their co-workers in the Mahbubnagar region today numbers some 60,000 members. It faces challenges aplenty. It also knows today remarkable growth prospects. On the one hand, the features of an urban and industrial, secular, technological developed and market-oriented world impinges more strongly now than ever before on some of the structures and ideas of Indian civilization, with the result that some of their integrating capacities have been undermined and voluntary organizations like the church provide platforms in social life alternate to the platforms traditional social forms in India have provided over the centuries. On the other, the invitations extended Christianity through the early work of missionaries, as portrayed in *Sepia Prints,* remain.

Kipling once implied that the meeting between East and West is at best problematic. Perhaps. But it has also proven extraordinarily productive, and it is in our modern world a meeting not only constant but also wonderfully stimulating.

Mom and Dad, like Mom's parents before them, were Mennonite missionaries in the Mahbubnagar region. The "prints" herein are some of the pictures, images and words that marked themselves upon Mom's mind and heart during a lifetime spent largely among Indians in India. *Sepia Prints*? A beautiful set reflecting the meeting of East and West through the life of one servant of God.

Paul D. Wiebe
Sociologist
Kodaikanal
June, 1989

For my Beloved John and all pioneer missionaries, many of whom died while on the Mission Field.

Left – Rev. and Mrs. John Pankratz
Center – Rev. and Mrs. N. Hiebert
Standing – Miss Elizabeth Neufeld

Miss Anna Suderman

Emboldened by the Lord's command to "Go preach, teach and heal," a preacher and his wife, the Rev. and Mrs. N.N. Hiebert, and a teacher, Miss Elizabeth Neufeld, went to India as Mennonite Brethren missionaries before the turn of the century.

The Hieberts stayed in India only eighteen months. They buried a child in India and then returned to America sick with malaria.

Anna Suderman, deaconess-nurse (who later became my third mother), had learned the Gujarathi language near Poona while working with the Christian Missionary Alliance mission. Hearing of the Mennonite Brethren beginning a mission in Hyderabad, she wrote to them and was accepted. She joined the J. Pankratzes (who had replaced the Hieberts) and Elizabeth Neufeld in Malkapet, Hyderabad.

Soon after the birth of their child, Daniel, my Father's parents Henry and Alvina (Starke) Bergthold and Daniel Bergthold, Father's grandfather, emigrated from Southern Russia to Minnesota.

They later moved to Colorado, then Kansas, Texas and finally settled in Oklahoma. My grandfather ministered in churches while farming, barely making enough income for his family.

Father was baptized when he was seventeen. He later studied in McPherson College, Kansas, and then in Light and Hope Bible School in Berne, Indiana. Dr. Torrey taught Father in Moody Bible Institute. Papa often quoted Dr. Torrey in his sermons.

In 1901, at a Mennonite Brethren conference in Ebenfeld, Kansas, Father was accepted as conference evangelist and traveled in the churches encouraging interest in foreign missions.

My Mother (back row, far right) with siblings and her parents Mr. and Mrs. Peter Mandtler, who in 1876 immigrated to Minnesota from Russia

Rev. and Mrs. Henry Bergthold, my Father's parents

While speaking in Dalmeny, Saskatchewan, Canada, Father noticed a beautiful, attentive woman who offered a prayer at the close of the service. His silent hope was that this woman, Katharina (Tiena), daughter of Mr. and Mrs. Peter Mandtler, was the one whom God had ordained for him.

Not long afterwards, Father wrote to the Mandtlers asking for Katharina's hand in marriage. They were married in June of 1902.

My Mother and Father on their wedding day, June 1902

Denkbaren Tochter. Katharina. Wandhar.

Jahrenbrunnhof den 1sten Januar 1892

Katharina, my Mother, made a white tucked dress for her wedding. This was contrary to the wish of the Mennonite minister who told her to wear the acceptable black dress befitting a prospective missionary. 1902

Father and Mother Bergthold's baptismal certificates, 1893 and 1895

Before leaving for mission work, my parents traveled extensively in the churches in the United States and Canada to interest the constituency in overseas missions.

During the sultry heat of August 1903, Father and Mother bumped over rough roads in horse-drawn buggies and trains. After reaching Buhler, Kansas, they were directed to a private home where I was born on August 17.

Continuing on their travels as soon as Mother was able, they pursued their visits until 1904 when they were ordained and commissioned in Mountain Lake, Minnesota, by Elder Heinrich Voth. In fall, with the blessings of the Mennonite Brethren Conference, they bid farewell and sailed for India from New York, not expecting to see parents or "home folks" for at least seven years.

Map of India prior to Independence c. 1940

A friend holding me on the *S.S. Cordillera*

India

"India, dark, dark India." Papa hummed the tune of this often sung mission hymn as we neared the shores of India in 1904. Father's religious zeal was intense and he was impatient to save the Indian people from "spiritual darkness and ignorance."

The oppressive August heat of Bombay shrouded us like a blanket. Father struggled to complete the necessary customs forms and purchased tickets for the three-day train journey to Hyderabad.

The jostling crowds and hungry urchins tugging at Papa's sleeves were a startling contrast from the relative comforts of the ship and his former experiences. Overwhelmed, he contended with the heavy luggage, appalled at the sight and thought of the thin, scantily clad men much smaller than himself asking to carry the larger pieces. He found us seats and then shoved our trunks and suitcases into the third class compartment to be rearranged when the train was in motion. Beggars solicited at the windows and mendicants extended their bowls for coins — the journey into India had begun.

Traveling in the train *bogie* with us was a *sadhu* (Hindu Holy man) who impressed Papa with his quiet composure. Father had read of the *sadhu* feats of endurance such as sleeping on nails, walking on fire and standing in one position for long periods of time in order to acquire spiritual merit. There was no chance, however, to communicate as neither Papa or the *sadhu* knew a word of the other's language. The hours passed as we watched the tranquil scenes of India slip by.

The journey ended at Hyderabad Station after three days and nights of traveling on wooden benches on the swaying train.

Coolies (porters) helped remove luggage from the train onto rickshaws pulled by men. Then we made our way through dusty streets and choking crowds to the bungalow of Rev. and Mrs. J.H. Pankratz in Malkapet.

HYDERABAD:
"The Face that launched a city".
Hyderabad's founder, Mohammed Quli Qutubshah, named the new city after his Hindu mistress Bhagmathi as Bhagnagar. Later, when Bhagmathi became Hydermahal, Bhagnagar became Hyderabad.

A Poem "Koh-i-stan"
"From the distance, thou didst appear barricaded in rocky aloofness
Timidly I crossed the rugged path, to find here, all of a sudden,
An open invitation in the sky, and friends' embrace in the air,
In an unknown land, the Voice that seemed ever known
Revealed to me a shelter of loving intimacy"
                Rabindranath Tagore
Hydrabad (as Tagore spelt it)
23-12-1933

As other missionaries had been required to do, Papa and Mama studied Telugu, one of the major languages spoken in the Deccan. A *munshi* taught them six or eight hours a day for one year using *Arden's Grammar* as the text.

The second year, fewer hours were spent with the *munshi* and the new missionaries traveled to the villages to practice the language they had learned.

Training was difficult and frustrating at times, particularly learning the verb endings and learning how to place the tongue in order to pronounce the difficult sounds.

Telugu *munshi* and his young wife

Papa inquired of the munshi *why a man on the street had looked blankly at him when he asked* bagunnara, *are you well? The teacher explained that the man was probably a villager, and would have responded to* bagunnau, *a more common form of the same word.*

The pioneer missionary group eating on the verandah of the Falaknuma Palace. Mother is seated to the right in front. Father took the picture.

Soon after we arrived in the Deccan, the *Nizam* (ruler) invited us, together with other missionaries, to the Falaknuma Palace in Hyderabad.

Elephants with their *mahouts* (elephant drivers) were sent to transport the group to the palace.

The Falaknuma Palace stands majestically on the crest of a hill and is reached by a small winding road. It was built at a cost of thirty-five lakhs by the late Sir Vigar-ul-Ulema and bought by the Nizam in 1897. The Nizam VI lived and died in the palace. Successive viceroys and the last Governor-General of India, Mr. C. Rajagopalachari, stayed in the palace.

Four hundred years ago what is now Hyderabad City was an area covered with granite stone hills, forest and a river flowing through.

The local governor, Sultan Quli Qutb Shah, started a little fort on top of a hill and called it Golconda. The Sultan established his own kingdom in 1518 with the breakdown of the ruling Bahamini and Golconda became a prosperous city. A bridge across the River Musi was constructed by the fourth ruler in 1573.

The city of Bhagyanagar was founded in 1591 on the southern bank of the River Musi. The story goes that the king chose the village called Chickalam as the spot for a new city on account of his love for a local Hindu dancing girl, Bhagmati, after whom the city was named.

In due course, the city acquired the name of Hyderabad. Misfortune befell the city with the conquest of the Deccan by the Moghul Emperor Aurangazeb in 1687. The headquarters of the Deccan then shifted to Aurangabad under the Moghul rule. In 1763, the Nizam shifted the headquarters back to Hyderabad and again the city flourished.

The British residency was established on the northern banks of the Musi River now referred to as Secunderabad and the gap between Hyderabad and Secunderabad gradually filled with residences and industry.

In the year 1802, Nawab Mir Alam built a reservoir. Construction was supervised by an Englishman, Mr. Russel. Water from the Mir Alam tank was channeled to the Purani Haveli Palace and others. Later, water was supplied to the public.

In September of 1908, the usually quiet Musi River rose in fury and struck the city with large scale destruction.

I remember Mother telling us in later years, how she and Elizabeth Neufeld took the boarding school children in pouring rain to higher ground. They huddled together on the hillock through the night and till the water receded the following day, when they returned to the school compound.

Sir M. Visveswarayya together with Ali Nawaz Jung proposed damming the river on its two tributaries, Musi and Easi, and channeling it as it passed through the city. Two reservoirs were thus formed in 1922 and 1927 and the new Hyderabad Water Works resulted.

The Deccan was a Muslim State ruled by H.E.H. the Nizam. Special stamps and currency known as *Halisika* minted in Hyderabad were used.

The first mint in Hyderabad was established at the old royal palace, Sultan Shahi in 1803. Almost a hundred years later, the mint was modernized and shifted to Saifabad.

The first Hali coins bearing the Charminar motif were silver rupee and four anna coins in 1904-1905. Nickel coinage for Hali came into vogue in 1919, when the round one-anna piece was minted.

Excerpts from "Press Reporter's Guild", Hyderabad

A typical "dak" bungalow.

Slowly the oxen-drawn carts plodded down the rutted roads. Villagers stopped their plowing or digging in the nearby fields to gaze at the unusual sight of *tellavaru* (white ones) traveling in oxcarts. Goats, sheep and buffalo nibbled at grass blades on the side of the road. Now and then children ran beside us.

In November 1904 when the stifling heat had given way to a cooler season, the Mennonite Brethren missionaries, now numbering six and three small children, were to join the Baptist missionary group in Nalgonda, eighty miles southeast of Hyderabad for a conference.

Nights en route were spent in *dak* bungalows (rest houses) which were used by travelers and were not always very clean. Toilet facilities were meager in these places. Water had to be brought from nearby wells or streams.

After the five-day conference, our family continued to Sooriapet, a distance of thirty miles, to visit the Baptist missionary family, A.J. Hueberts. While in Sooriapet, Mother became dangerously ill with smallpox. ("Put your complete faith in God alone," the Mennonite Brethren Board had instructed us. None of us had been vaccinated against any disease.)

Mother's fever rose higher every day. She couldn't bear the weight of her heavy hair, so her thick, brown braid was cut off. Everything humanly possible was done to alleviate her suffering. I was not allowed to see my Mother and cried uncontrollably while she lay dying and Father prayed in anguish.

Rev. A.J. Huebert carried me to a nearby field to quiet my cries when quite suddenly, my screams stopped, apparently the same moment Mother's soul went to her Savior.

I was one year and three months old. At the graveside, Dr. J.S. Timpany, who had been summoned from Hyderabad, prayed, "Lord, let this small child, Viola, grow up to serve Thee in the work her Mother had to leave so early."

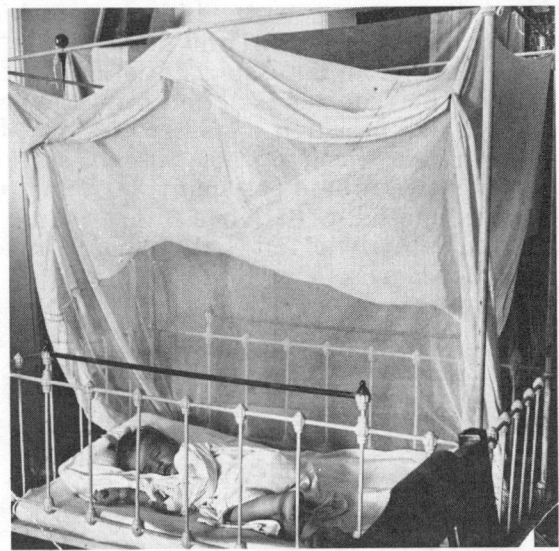

Maggie *ayah* (nurse) helped care for me after mother's death.

After wearing heavy gold earrings for many years, Maggie's earlobes stretched almost to her shoulders.

Anna Epp, who had come from Russia to India with the American Baptist Mission, joined my Father in marriage in 1905.

Half the mission staff was single women. Five *missammas*, as they were called, lived in the same stations with the married missionary couples and early on, in the same bungalows. Some, in the Indian community, thought that the *missammas* were the *doras'* mistresses.

The Rev. A. Huebert family on the right, my Father, my new Mother and I in Sooriapet

In 1907, it was time to "enlarge the place of thy tent — lengthen thy cords and strengthen thy stakes." (Is. 54:2)

With these directions in mind, Rev. J. Pankratz and Papa made an extended tour to the south of Hyderabad, stopping their ox-carts at many villages and preaching the gospel. As they proceeded, they reached the village of Nagarkurnool.

Choosing a rocky hillock on which to camp, they surveyed the surrounding territory. A site for a mission station was obtained after the required sanction from the government was procured.

There was no other mission station for thirty-five miles. The many surrounding villages offered a challenge to my young, energetic Father who felt that he should invest his life for Christ.

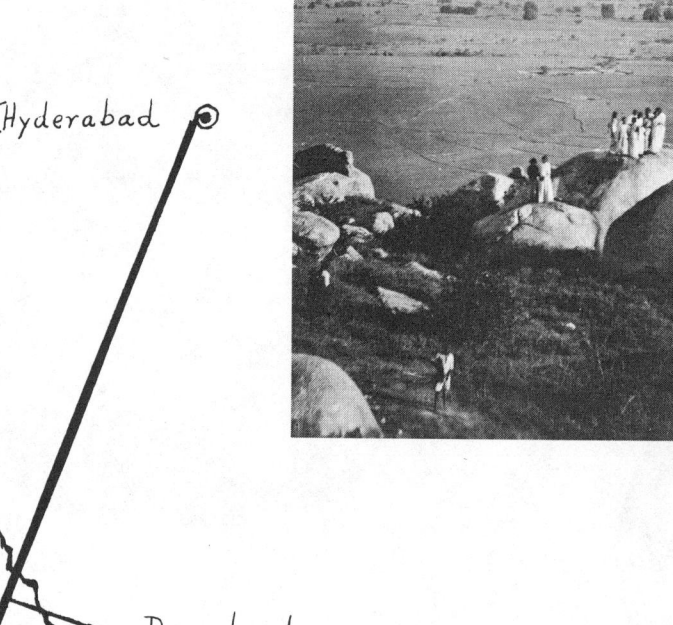

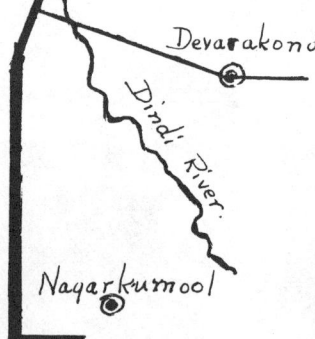

Within a year, sister Lydia was born. The four of us moved the eighty miles from Hyderabad to the hillock about a mile from the Nagarkurnool village and moved into a tent under a *Kordipilla Chettu* (Rain Tree).

In early years, dress codes were strictly maintained. Dressing us little girls in many clothes must have seemed absurd to the ayah, whose own children ran around almost naked in the sunshine.

The *topee* (pith helmet) was compulsory headgear from sunup to sundown for fear of sunstroke.

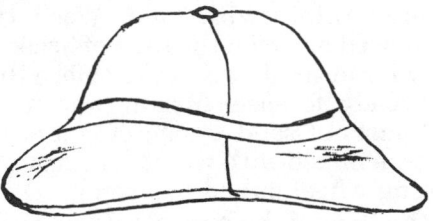

Indian women covered their heads with shawls or the ends of their *saris* and sometimes the men placed green leaves under their turbans to prevent the sun from beating on their heads.

During the noon hour, there was a hush except for the buzzing of gnats and flies as everyone sought the shade of a tree or wall.

We wore cholera belts during the rainy season when the dreaded cholera usually reached epidemic proportions. It was thought that keeping the stomach warm would prevent the illness from attacking the system.

My sister, Lydia and I, wore several petticoats over pantaloons covered by dresses made from handwoven cloth. We were encouraged to wear shoes and stockings out-of-doors to prevent scorpion and insect bites.

Missionaries and other foreigners living in India, continued wearing layers of western clothing despite uncomfortable weather conditions.

I knit my own cholera belt at age ten.

I held onto Mother's skirt as she struggled to push up the flapping, soggy canvas of the tent. Father dashed out into the driving rain and drove the stakes deeper into rocky ground to tighten the tent ropes.

The heavy wind howled and pulled at the straining ropes. Once in a while, a gust of rain splashed us. Shivering, we waited out this storm just as we had done for so many others.

Weeks of living in the tent turned into months as Father organized the construction of the one-story bungalow in which we would live.

Trenches three to four feet deep were dug; the foundation was then filled in with crushed brick and rock chips. The walls, about eighteen inches thick, were built with locally made bricks. The bricks were made with mud and water mixed the day before, then poured into wooden moulds, pressed down well by hand and leveled. The mud mould was then removed and the brick dried in the sun for five or six days before firing. The sun-dried bricks were piled carefully to be fired and plastered thinly with mud. Wood that had been placed between the rows of bricks burned slowly for at least two weeks before the bricks were ready for use. Mortar was made with eight parts of sand to one of *chunam* (lime). This was mixed with water and ground by the grinding wheel pulled by oxen.

The floor of the bungalow was built about four feet above ground level. Women carried the stones and bricks to the men for construc-

tion and carried water from a well some distance away.

After several months, two rooms of the house were nearly complete. As soon as the roof was finished we moved our camp cots and chairs into one end of a large room. The cow with her newborn calf were tied to the other side of the room together with the goat. Chickens were placed under a basket and the cat shared my cot. During the first night, heavy rain loosened some bricks from the wall. They fell and killed the calf. Pushing our cots against the wall, we piled what belongings we could on the beds and chairs to keep them from getting wet in the ankle-deep water.

Father continued encouraging the builders and slowly progress was made towards completing the bungalow.

I was on the verandah with my sister Lydia watching cook Abram carry savory fried chicken on a platter when a kite swooped down and carried off a large portion of the meat. This was not the first time something like this had happened. The cookhouse was some distance away from the bungalow. The food was brought from the kitchen to the dining room or to the back verandah where suppers were eaten during the cooler season.

Any leftover food was given away or put into a small screened cupboard. The legs of the cupboard stood in earthen saucers filled with water to discourage ants and other vermin from crawling into the food.

All water for drinking was boiled and then poured into and stored in large earthen pots to cool.

Screened cupboard, and earthen *kujas*, water pots, in which our drinking water was cooled

A mail runner brought our foreign mail from Janampett. He carried a pole extended over his shoulder with a locked canvas bag on one end and a tinkling bell on the other. The mailman trotted the forty miles once a week. His return was eagerly awaited both for his safety and the mail which was often several months en route.

Boys eager to earn school fees, swept leaves, ran errands, cleaned oil lamps and took *chits* (messages) from one place to another. Telephones were unknown and written messages were our means of communication.

The *dergi*, as the tailor was called, was glad to earn a better wage than he received elsewhere. He squatted on the verandah on a mat with his own hand-manipulated Singer sewing machine. He could reproduce a pattern exactly, including the patch which had been on the old garment.

The *dhobi* (laundryman) or his wife took our clothes to the nearest pond or stream and scrubbed and beat them clean on the rocks. Clothes were spread on the ground and dried in the hot sun, folded and brought to the house where the *dhobi* carefully and patiently ironed each piece with his heavy charcoal iron. Buttons which hadn't broken with the pounding on the rocks were likely to lose their places as the iron box passed over them.

Papa hired a horse-drawn tonga in which to travel around Hyderabad. He left his bicycle at the mission home of the Pankratzes until he needed it for the return trip to Nagarkurnool.

Because oxcart travel took too long Papa cycled to the city to get money to pay the workers and to buy construction supplies. He brought back bags of coins because paper money was not minted in those days.

There were times when *dongalu* (thieves) tried to stop him during the eighty mile trip which took him two days, but he cycled faster than they could run.

Once after an especially tiring day of cycling in the heat and dust with a heavy bag of coins, he could go no further. Though he could see the bungalow in the distance, he stopped near a small bridge and making sure no one was watching, he put his bicycle with the money under some leaves and walked home across the country.

Early the next morning, Benjamin, a trusted helper, was sent to bring back the bicycle and bag of money.

Above – The Nagarkurnool Mission Station buildings surrounded by a brick wall

Dormitories for school girls and boys were built as well as housing for workers. Then a church and school were constructed and later a hospital. A deep well provided enough water for gardens and those residing on the compound.

Waking from sleep before the first light of a new day, Papa climbed the ladder to what we called his *prophet's chamber,* a room which was added to the roof upstairs. Here he found solace as he studied his beloved Bible, and books in Hebrew, Greek, German, Telugu, and English.

During the hottest months, we slept on the flat roof where Papa studied the stars. He was fascinated by the heavens and studied books on astronomy ordered from England.

In 1910, Papa awakened us at about two o'clock in the morning to witness the spectacular appearance of Halley's Comet. Though I was only seven years old, I can remember that Heavenly body with its tail which seemed to reach the earth. "I wonder if the star which led the wise men to Bethlehem was any more beautiful than this?" Papa said.

The bedroom I shared with my three sisters (on the right side of the picture above) was large and airy. The thick walls and high ceilings of the rooms with deep verandahs adjacent to them kept the bungalow cooler. Doors were closed at sundown to prevent snakes and other unwanted creatures from entering the house.

Left: A corner of our living room in Nagarkurnool from which the bed can be seen. Note the *welsh hat* (chamber pot) under the bed.

Our furniture was purchased from other missionaries, now and then from a British official, or was locally made.

A charcoal drawing I made of the Nagarkurnool home.

Pioneer missionaries: Papa and Mama to the far left, John and Marie Pankratz, John and Mary Voth, at a meeting in Nagarkurnool

Father advanced money to preachers so that they could purchase plots of land. He encouraged them to farm so they could supplement their meager income and become more self-sufficient.

Church congregations were taught to tithe ten percent of their income to help with the church budget.

The church elders, preachers and teachers from the villages and compound with Father.

The *rumaalu* (turban) worn by our clergy was not removed except in church or at a religious meeting

Nagarkurnool tank (reservoir) where we sometimes walked for an outing and waded in the water. Papa carried a cane to ward off snakes and yapping dogs. Tiger Hill, seen in the background, was said to have tigers on it but we saw only leopards sunning themselves on the rocks.

Mama made the area surrounding the bungalow verdant and green. She placed rows of clay pots, filled with herbs, roses and tropical plants, along the edges of the verandah.

Many of the vegetables Mama grew in the garden were used for the dormitory children's curries. Tomatoes were considered poisonous until Mama introduced them. She dried and distributed seeds to those interested in planting tomatoes in their own gardens.

Each day school boys filled the *ouzu* (water trough) from the large hand-dug well from which they carried water to the potted plants and garden.

Mama was a good story teller and took time to teach us German songs, reading and writing despite being responsible for many other things. She supervised the houseparents of boarding children, including their food and their health care, and taught the older children how to mend and sew their clothes.

After Dr. K.L. Schellenberg moved to Shamshabad Station, Mama managed the hospital built adjacent to the bungalow. She trained some Telugu women to help her. The hospital was the only medical facilty available for miles around except for villagers, who, for a fee, dispensed herbal remedies.

The hospital

Touring

After the monsoon rains had stopped and before it got too hot, we toured surrounding villages to give the message of Hope.

Two sturdy well-fed oxen pulled the first oxcart and a caravan of others followed. One carried the preachers and their wives; the next contained the large tent which included the outer tent with awning, inner tent and bath enclosure. Other carts with more tents and supplies followed over rocky, rutted roads and sometimes muddy fields. At times we rode in a horse-drawn *tonga* (carriage) or walked behind the carts. Father usually rode his horse ahead or behind the caravan. One day he was thrown from his horse while riding near a village. A man came running to us shouting that *the tella dora* (white man) lies unconscious in the sun. A cart was quickly sent to get Father. By the time they brought him back, he was conscious, but Mother was convinced that his periodic dizzy spells originated that day.

At noon, the caravan stopped to rest the oxen and horses and give the people time to cook *chapatis* (flat bread). Then slowly, slowly the oxen plodded on until evening when we found a suitable place to set up camp.

A rest stop under a tree
near newly painted shrines

Abram, our cook, prepared rice while the delicious smell of *dahl* (lentils) drifted from the blackened pot on the campfire. We carried most of our fuel for cooking as Papa did not like his food prepared over a cow-chip fire. Sometimes, if wood was not available, we were able to find straw or kaffir cornstalks.

Rising early with the sun, we packed our *saamaan* (belongings) on the carts to complete the journey. Our destination was one of the major villages in Nagarkurnool District from where the preachers would be able to walk to the surrounding smaller villages. When we reached the outskirts of Telkapalli, Father approached the village headman to ask permission to set up the camp and to conduct meetings.

The greater part of the village population came to watch the proceedings of setting up our tents under the shade of a Neem tree. "Why bring your water?" the villagers asked. "We can bring you some from our wells and cow-chips to cook with."

While Papa and the preachers put up the tents and spread rice straw on the ground inside the tents to discourage snakes, Mama dispensed medicine and bandaged sores. We children toured the campsite and did small errands. Children from the village touched our skin and stroked our fair hair, surprised that we could converse in Telugu.

As evening approached, lanterns were lit and the kerosene pressure petromax was prepared for the meeting. Villagers threaded their way among those already seated to find a place to squat. Some brought a mat to sit on. Mangy dogs wandered everywhere, babies fussed and cried. Closely packed together, the villagers exuded the combined odor of garlic and spices, and coconut oil if their earnings were sufficient to use it to smooth down their hair, and the sweet scent of faded marigolds and jasmine.

The crowd quieted down as the preachers sang and drummed. Papa showed stereoptician slides of the Life of Christ in a large enclosure. He made the *magic lantern* as it was called, by fashioning a box with lenses from England. For light, he used a petromax lamp and projected the slides onto a large sheet. While the pictures were being shown, Father was pelted with cowdung and stones by a group of young men standing at the back. A frail, little old woman rose from the floor and stood in front of Papa. Pointing her finger at the miscreants, she shouted, "My sons, you'll throw not one more stone except over my dead body. This man is telling us of the love of God. We haven't heard this before. Sit down or get out."

Age was respected and the old woman's words heeded.

My sisters and I were glad when the meeting ended. We ran back to our tent and crawled under the mosquito nets onto our cots, too tired even to whisper. A log fire was kept burning all night and we watched the flames dance, imagining eyes of prowling jackals or panthers.

Cow-chips for fuel, ready to sell

On another night, some men told the preachers accompanying us, "Tonight we are going to burn you and your tents down." Aware of potential problems, Father had fires built near each tent and we took turns watching and praying until dawn. The following day, our camp was dismantled and we moved to another location a day's journey away.

Permission to reside in India needed to be obtained every year.

Form No. 225—Consular.
(October, 1916.)

Extended for one year from date of expiration.

Lucien Memminger,
American Consul

Certificate of Registration at Madras, India, June 24, 1918.

This document is not a passport and is intended for local use. It is good for one year and may be renewed once by this office if presented when it is about to expire.

AMERICAN CONSULAR SERVICE,

Madras, India, May 28, 1917.
(Place and date.)

This is to Certify, That Daniel F. Bergthold whose signature is subscribed hereto, has been registered in this office as an American citizen by authority of the Department of State at Washington.

The following members of his family reside with him:

Wife: Anna Sudermann Bergthold
(Name.)

Children by previous marriage:
Viola Bergthold — Aug. 17, 1903 Nagarku
Lydia Bergthold — Mar. 3, 1907
Bertha Bergthold — Aug. 31, 1908
Martha Bergthold — Oct. 16, 1909
Henry Bergthold — Sep. 5, 1915
Samuel — Oct. 21, 1918

PERSONAL D[ESCRIPTION]

Age: 41 years
Height: five feet,
Color of eyes: brown
Color of hair: brown
Complexion: dark
Distinguishing features
right eye.

[SEAL]
(Fee one dollar.)

$1

Consul

D. F. Bergthold
(Signature of person registered.)

During the hot weather, passengers were allowed, when the sea was calm, to take some bedding and sleep on deck. Everything was removed at dawn so that the lascars could sluice down the decks. Quoits, shuffleboard, deck tennis, and other games were played after breakfast. At times races were organized to relieve the monotony of the long journey.

On Sundays there were religious services, often chaired by the captain, attended by passengers, officers, and sailors (off duty). Meal times were fun! Children ate before adults.
Grown-ups "dressed" for dinner, then after eating, went to the lounges for programs, or to read and write, or converse with others.

Father, my sisters and I had never seen Mother's parents who lived in Russia. After a steamship trip from Bombay to Trieste in 1912, we disembarked and traveled to Tiege, Blumenort, Kronsgart, Waldheim and Gnadenau, to visit churches and become acquainted with Mother's relatives.

While our parents continued visiting churches, we four sisters stayed with our Epp grandparents in Rosenort. The irises and tulips grew profusely along the pathways up to the *shoene* barn which was attached to their dwelling. Grandma Epp kept the *borscht* steaming all day in huge cauldrons on the wood stove to feed the farm workers and family.

We studied our lessons in German in the local school for six months. The instructor was harsh and often scolded the girls and spanked the boys.

Our next destination was America. My sister Lydia and I began our first formal English education in another one-room school in Corn, Oklahoma, where our grandparents, the Rev. Henry Bergtholds, lived. Our teacher was a son of the instructor who taught us in Russia.

After half a year of experiencing American culture, attending numerous family gatherings and church functions, we boarded a ship back to India.

One night fire broke out in a cabin opposite ours in which Catholic Sisters slept. The nuns, dressed in bright red flannel petticoats, rushed out to escape the blaze. My sisters and I giggled as we saw such a contrast to their somber black habits, before Mama pushed us back into our cabin. The fire was soon contained and the Sisters returned to their beds.

The passenger liner on which we had traveled for a few weeks, docked at Ballard Pier in Bombay. There, shipping agents came abroad and for a fee, helped us through customs and assisted us to the waiting train that took us to Hyderabad. From there, we traveled by oxcart back to our home, Nagarkurnool.

Lydia and I dressed for school.

Central Station in Madras was hot and bustling. Our ongoing train left in the evening so we had a full day in the city. We washed and changed our clothes in the first class waiting room before visiting Moore Market which had every conceivable type of merchandise under one roof. After a swim in the sea, we ate a three course meal at Spencer's Restaurant at Egmore Station. The restaurant had white tablecloths and real silver cutlery. After this we boarded the train for Metupalliam.

Early the next morning, we rolled up our bedding, gathered our possessions and peered eagerly from the windows to catch a glimpse of the cog-train that would take us to the "Queen of Hill Stations," Ootacamund or Ooty.

The journey up the *ghat* (mountain road) was breathtaking and the air 8000 feet above sea level was exhilarating. It was so very cool despite the brilliant sunlight. Putting on our jerseys, we gazed with delight at the rushing waterfalls and the dense, blue Eucalyptus groves which we saw in the distance. The Niligiri Hills were named after the Blue Gum or Eucalyptus trees.

Traveling from Nagarkurnool to the Niligiri Hills took three days. Venkaya drove the oxen pulling our cart the first forty miles. The oxen were coaxed and prodded with a stick. Venkaya twisted the oxens' tails to make them move a little faster. If they still didn't move fast enough, he bit their tails. This made Lydia and me scream, so he didn't use this method very often.

On reaching Krishna Railway Station, bedrolls, water *kujas* (earthen jugs), food baskets and steel trunks were loaded into a third class compartment of the train. Normally one of the fathers or mothers from the surrounding mission stations escorted the group. This time, Mama was the adult escort. She scrubbed the seats and sides of the compartment with Lysol and water before we were allowed to unpack and spread our bedding. We turned the fans on full speed, which really only redistributed the heat, then settled down for a long, hot, but fun train ride. The train stopped frequently and we got out of the carriage to look around and watch the vendors.

Wellington Viaduct, Nilgiri Railway

Arriving in Ooty, we hired a cart for our luggage. The little children rode on top of the bedrolls while the rest of us trudged behind the cart to the missionary residence, Grace House. After a few days, we took another cog-train for Coonoor.

Perhaps Kipling reflected the attitude of many foreigners in India with a statement from ***Plain Tales From the Hills***. "A man should, whatever happens, keep to his own caste, race and breed."

British schools were started in the hills for expatriate children of tea planters, businessmen and missionaries. Indians were not allowed. By the time I attended Hebron, a few Anglo-Indians were admitted. Perhaps this was because the fathers of these children could afford expensive tuition and boarding costs. Father and Mother scrimped and saved in order to pay our school fees.

My sister, Lydia, and I were sent to Hebron, a British boarding school in Coonoor high in the Niligiri Hills of South India in 1913.

Hebron was a school for girls and very young boys who had sisters in boarding. Breeks in Ootacamund was a school for boys. Most British civil servants sent their children to school in England at a very young age.

Maths, British and Indian History, Geography, French, Latin, arts and needlework were some of the subjects taught. Sports included tennis, badminton, field hockey and Indian clubs.

Breeks School was the center where students from several schools gathered for final examinations. Results for Trinity in Music, and Cambridge for Academics were known only when results were returned from England.

CAMBRIDGE UNIVERSITY JUNIOR LOCAL EXAMINATION
JULY AND DECEMBER 1920

CENTRE Ootacamund
Name of Student Viola Catherine Berg...
Index-number
Place of Examination Breek's Memorial School, Ootacamund

A final outing in the beautiful Government Gardens, before our parents and Martha returned to the plains, and Lydia, Bertha and I to boarding school

We could hear the high, thin voice of the matron in charge saying, "An ounce of castor oil and orange juice will purge away any impurities you may have brought with you." It would take more than her encouragement to persuade us that this dreaded concoction was good for us. There were five or six *chatties* in each bathroom. A long queue of girls stood outside each bathroom after the castor oil purge. The sweepers, whose task it was to empty the portable pots, were kept busy.

We were instructed to bathe twice a week. Hot water was heated in large kerosene tins over wood fires and brought to the bathing room at five or ten minute intervals. There was barely enough time to sit in the tin tub to scrub or be scrubbed before it was the next person's turn.

Ten or twelve of us slept in one dormitory room. The older ones monitored baths and prayers for the younger ones.

The principal, Miss E. Chaplain, was a sweet, understanding person but some of the other teachers and matrons were inordinately strict.

Rules were strictly enforced. Children who wet their beds had to wash their linens and stand in the sun with the wet mattress on their heads for part of the morning.

"Don't" rules were numerous:
"Don't talk with the servants."
"Don't talk in study hall."
"Don't talk after lights out."
"Don't whistle."
"Don't sleep with your hands under the covers." This was to discourage us from masturbating.

Ivy cried in class one day because she did not understand the sums in arithmetic. The teacher told her she was a baby and made her lie on the floor and suck on a pacifier. This incident as well as other similar unnecessary punishments annoyed all of us. Many times we thought we should defend our rights but were frightened into submission that the same fate might befall us.

Our meals were served at long tables. Soup, bread and *scrape* (butter) or jam spread on the bread and scraped off, was our regular fare for the evening meal; while the teachers at each end of the table enjoyed roast and potatoes.

When we became too boisterous, the matron in charge put us on "silence." We became considerably quieter but still communicated in sign language.

My monthly allowance was, like everyone else's, four annas which was a quarter of a rupee or thirty-five cents. I kept one anna for Sunday collection and with the rest bought a bun or other edibles from the *bazaar* (market), where we were allowed to go once a week. Now and then we each contributed an anna towards a tin of sweetened condensed milk for a forbidden "midnight feast." After the matron had made her last rounds, we slipped out of the bathroom door into the woods nearby and ate our clandestine meal.

One night, one of the kitchen staff saw us sneak out of the dormitory. We threatened him that if he would tell on us, we would tell the matron that he was planning to steal (many of our mackintoshes had just been stolen). Why else would he be around the premises late at night?

The only time we saw boys was in church or when we took our examinations at Breeks, the boys' boarding school. Sometimes we wrote letters to each other and hid them in the hollows of trees for the boys to find — prearranged by the sisters of the boys to whom we wrote.

During World War I, British *tommies* (soldiers) vacationed in the Niligiri Hills. Some of the soldiers got our names and wrote to us asking for our pictures. I replied with a picture of a *toda* (local tribeswoman) and never received a reply.

Drama in school was great fun. We enacted many of Shakespeare's plays and enjoyed dressing up. Although always with a chaperone, we hiked and explored the beautiful hills, gathering wild flowers which we later pressed. Best of all, we enjoyed Girl Guiding and our adored captain, Gladys Groves.

Girl Guides drilling, and our captain Gladys Groves

It was a sunny afternoon, in 1915, in Coonoor. We were having an afternoon "sing" when the principal, our beloved Miss Chaplin, called Lydia, Bertha and me aside and said, "I have a surprise for you. Go to Brooklands (a missionary rest house in Coonoor). Your Father has come to see you."

Most parents came up to the Hills in early summer to escape the depressing stifling heat of the plains. My parents had been up in May, so we were surprised to hear Father had come up in September.

We ran down the slopes of the tea plantation between the school premises and Brooklands, to find Father awaiting us. After hugs and kisses, Papa said, "I have come to tell you that you have a new baby brother," to which we chorused, "Good, and how is Mama?"

He replied with tears in his voice, "Two weeks ago Mama went to be with her Lord where I know she is all right."

We wept bitterly together, while Papa told us of the heavy rains and the *Nalla Vagu* (Black River) which had been in spate. Doctor Booker, who lived forty miles away, had not been able to cross the swollen river. Mama, assisted only by Lucamma whom she had trained, delivered her fifth child, Abraham, but soon after bled to death with postpartum hemorrhage.

Papa and a carpenter used a door and a *punkah* (wooden fan) to make a coffin, while other loving hands dug the grave behind the house.

After the high river receded, Papa took Martha, Henry and the newborn baby to be cared for by missionary Anna Suderman in Hyderabad before he came to Coonoor to tell us the sad news of Mother's death.

Miss Anna Suderman (who later became our mother) holding five-month old Abie on her lap, and Martha and Henry near her. Mary, barely visible, behind her with helpers.

Mother Anna Epp-Bergthold's grave, September 5, 1915.

Nearly three months later, we went to our motherless home for Christmas. The school children and teachers in Nagarkurnool welcomed us home with garlands and did all they could to make it a happy vacation, but there was an ache in our hearts. We missed our mother. We made each other gifts for Christmas and from Papa we received small suitcases and Bibles to take back to school.

Our little brother, Abe, died of malaria six months after Mother had died and after we had returned to boarding school.

Papa married Anna Suderman in June, 1916, in a simple, beautiful ceremony in a small Tamil church in Ooty.

Anna had come to India under the Christian Missionary Alliance and was studying Gujarathi near Poone when the Mennonite Brethren Mission started in Hyderabad. She applied to the Mennonite Brethren Board and was asked to join the Telugu work in Hyderabad.

My sisters and I loved this pretty, gentle lady and told Papa "we would like to have her as our Mother."

Christmas, 1916, was a happy holiday. Lydia and I, along with twenty Indian children, were baptized in an ouzu *(water trough) in the garden. The preachers who had come for refresher meetings and to see our new Mother helped carry water to the* ouzu *in* kundas *(earthen pots) from a well a mile away. The well that was nearby, had run dry.*

In October, 1918, Mama gave birth to Samuel. "For this child I prayed." Her own, but so were we. She never showed favor to any of us. I never heard her grumble. When we complained about something, Papa said, "Try to be like Mama who finds something good in everything."

Our new Mama never tired of helping us and those around her in the hospital, school or in the villages. She loved gardening and planted avocado, grapefruit, lemon and orange trees alongside mango, banana and papayas in the garden a mile from the compound where a deep well provided ample water after the well in the compound had run dry.

Elizabeth Voth with us, her Bergthold friends

Our new brother, Samuel on my lap, surrounded by his other siblings

We had no electric fans or lights in Nagarkurnool. Despite the thick walls of the bungalow, shutting out the heat was a problem. It helped to use *khaskhas tatties* (fine grass mats) across the doors and windows. These mats were sprayed with water from time to time which gave us some relief.

Punkahs hung in the dining room and two bedrooms. A *punkah* was a twelve foot board covered with matting and a cloth frill. It was attached to the ceiling with ropes and pulled to and fro to circulate the hot air. Sometimes the monotony of pulling the ropes put the man pulling to sleep; other times, the man lay on the mat on the verandah with the rope attached to his foot, pumping up and down, acceptant of his menial task.

The bungalow verandah was resplendent with potted plants such as elephant ears, ferns and creepers climbing up the pillars. Pots and boxes were used as they were easy to water and could be kept in the shade if necessary.

Our evening meals were often on the verandah after sundown, concerted by a flock of mynah birds settling down into the tamarind tree for the night. The heavy sweet scent of frangipani, oleander and Queen of the Night blossoms filled the air. Then, quite suddenly, the tropical night spread its inky blackness over the land. Myriads of tiny winged bugs clustered around the warm light of the kerosene lantern. After prayers Papa would say, "Zu bet, schlaft suesz. Gott befohlen" ("To bed, sleep well. God Bless").

A common sight along the ancient tree-lined roads was cattle being herded homeward as the shadows lengthened.

Monkeys swinging from the branches, colored birds and crows darted to and fro. A few alighted on the backs of the cattle searching for ticks or flies.

Before the Hook Festival was banned by the British, Father took these pictures while we watched in horrified fascination.

A man, who had chosen to sacrifice himself to the gods, stood stoically while a huge iron hook was jabbed into his back. He was then fastened to a long bamboo pole which was hoisted onto the top of the Jaggernaut Temple Wagon. There he swung, (see picture below), while the cart was pulled by many men through the rutted village streets.

Crowds crushed together straining to watch. After hours in the heat, the cart was brought to a halt and the man, now in a stupor, was taken down and the hook removed from his back.

The Jaggernaut chariot of the god Vishnu who exacts blind devotion and terrible sacrifice

Towards evening, Ramakka came running to tell Mother that a patient had been brought from the Amarabad Hills, forty miles away. I went with Mama and saw a poor badly mauled seven year old boy lying in a cloth hammock.

The men carrying the boy told us that the boy's family had been sleeping outside their hut when screams awakened them. They saw a tiger dragging the child by his head and gave chase with sticks, kettles and drums. The men beat off the tiger and brought the child back to the village where the women were lamenting and weeping. The boy had lost both his ears and much of his scalp and the villagers applied soft cowdung on the wounds to try and stop the bleeding.

The child was then carried for two days in the heat and dust to "the doctor with kind hands in Nagarkurnool."

Mama's helpers, seeing the gruesome sight, fled. Seeing her aides disappear, Mama turned to me saying, "You have always wanted to be a doctor, I need your help." Wave after wave of nausea swept over me as I helped Mama clean away the cowdung and crusted blood. We gave the child sips of milk and water and an injection and then wrapped his head in bandages and put him to bed on a clean sheet.

Much prayer, patient care and medicine helped the boy survive. Months later, he returned to his home in the Amarabad Hills.

Sixty years later, I asked S. Abraham, an evangelist who traveled in many villages, if he had ever seen a man without ears in the Amarabad Hills. His eyes lit up as he said that he had met a man near Munanur with terrible scars and no ears. The man had told Abraham that he had been saved by the kind hands in the mission hospital and that he had become a Christian.

A group of villagers from the hill country

Early pictures taken by my Father

Picking lice out of each other's hair

Chinna pillalu, small children

Father was one of the first to use audio-visual materials in reporting work on the mission field to audiences in America and in presenting Bible truths to congregations in India. He was an avid amateur photographer and taught himself the processing of films.

With personal money, my parents bought a handset printing press and Father taught himself and interested students how to set type, cut and print. The Telugu periodical *Suvarthamani* (Gospel News) and *The Harvest Field* for English readers were printed and distributed.

Papa also founded the Bethany Bible School where many men and women were trained to shepherd the ever growing number of members in the churches. Because many of the wives were illiterate, adult literacy classes were taught so the women could learn to read and help educate their children.

The first *agni bandy* (fire-cart) most people had ever seen, and the first car in the Mission. No more ox-carts! At least not on the big roads.

Book 2

1921 - 1936

Surrounded by my three sisters

"Don't forget to write," I tearfully said, hugging my boarding school chums as we bid farewell to Ootacamund.

After the three-day train journey to Nagarkurnool, we again went through the goodbyes and tears with our Indian friends.

The six-week ship journey in 1921 passed quickly. Landing in New York, we traveled by train to Oklahoma City and then on to Corn, Oklahoma, where our grandparents, the Rev. and Mrs. Henry Bergthold, lived. My sisters and I attended school while living in the small house our parents rented. During the summer months, all of us visited churches together.

From an intercultural, interdenominational girls' school in India, we found ourselves in a tight, closely-knit community in America. We felt very conspicuous as daughters of missionaries and were closely scrutinized. The fashions my sisters and I wore were out of date and we were sometimes ridiculed. After a church performance one evening, one of my cousins told me that I really should wear proper underwear. I was mortified.

It never occurred to us that India was not our home. America, the land of plenty, was the place our relatives lived. We needed to become reacquainted. They were not familiar with distant cultures and places and we were unfamiliar with their farm procedures, livestock and everyday living, but we learned.

We owned little as a family but what we had, had to be auctioned before returning to India. Among these things was a red leather writing case which Mama had used for years. Someone offered one dollar for the writing case. I was so upset I bid five dollars even though I didn't have the money. Papa, touched, gave the writing case to me with love.

My chums from Hebron, the Girls' School in the Niligiri Hills, India, and I kept up close correspondence. Eva Painter was one of these special friends who went to England for further studies.

She wrote me the following excerpt taken from a letter dated 15 February 1922:

> St Bruno's.
> 1 Banbury Rd.
> Oxford.
> Feb. 15th 22
>
> My dearly beloved Orlochee
>
> ".... Wael, to change the subject again, is'nt it *foolish* of Midge to have bobbed her hair? I'm going to write and tell her that I think her quite, quite mad. I want awfully to see what you look like with your hair done up in two funny little sticky-out lumps, just over your ears, as your lovely drawings showed! It looked awful funny, but I guess really you look quite respectable
>
> Your loving chum Eva

A photo of me with my hair coiled over my ears, as mentioned above. It was considered quite risqué to bob one's hair, as our Scottish friend "Midge" Angus had done.

One of my friends in Corn, Oklahoma was told to leave the church till her hair grew again, after "bobbing" her hair.

It was a cold, misty day when Lydia and I said a tearful goodbye to Papa and Mama. It would be six or seven years before we would see our beloved parents again.

Lydia was fourteen and I was eighteen. We had enrolled in Tabor Academy, Hillsboro, Kansas, in the fall of 1921, a few days before Papa and Mama left. Our younger brothers and sisters were still young enough to accompany our parents back to India.

Friends accompanied Lydia, far left, and me, third from the right, to the Hillsboro Railway depot, when we said goodbye to our parents in 1921.

Tina Franz and I, after we won the tennis tournament

Tabor College did not have a tennis court. Anxious to play tennis, my girl friends and I obtained permission to mark out a court. We started removing the grass and raking the area on which to play, when two young men walked by. "Give me your hoe and let me help," one of them said.

To this I replied, "Get your own and come and work."

As the men left one asked the other, "Who was that girl?"

"That was the Bergthold girl," was his companion's response.

"A girl?" was John Wiebe's surprised remark, "I thought missionary Bergthold was referring to his sons when he told us to take care of his children at the farewell meeting. I promised myself I would take care of them."

John, who became my fiancé, was born on 29 March 1900 to Abram and Susana Wiebe in Carson, Minnesota. His father was pastor of the local Mennonite Brethren Church for forty years.

John's parents had migrated to America from Russia about the same time my grandparents had.

Father and Mother Wiebe

Below – John's birth certificate

No. 027—Certified Copy of Birth Register in Cottonwood County, State of Minnesota. Class 4

No.	DATE OF BIRTH			NAME, IF ANY	SEX (and Condition, as Twins, Illegitimate, etc.)	COLOR
	Month	Day	Year			
11	3	29	1900	Johann Wiebe	Male	White

PLACE OF BIRTH OF CHILD (Town or City)	FULL CHRISTIAN NAME OF EACH PARENT
Carson Twp.	Abram Wiebe, father
	Susana Wiebe, mother

BIRTHPLACE OF EACH PARENT (Give the State or Nation)	OCCUPATION OF FATHER	WHEN REGISTERED		
		Month	Day	Year
Russia	Farming	1	19	1901

STATE OF MINNESOTA,
County of Cottonwood

IN DISTRICT COURT OF SAID COUNTY

I, M. B. Severson, Clerk of the District Court in and for said County and State, do hereby certify that the foregoing is a full and complete transcript of the entries appearing of record in the Register of Births now remaining in my said office relating to the birth of the said Johann Wiebe and of the whole thereof.

WITNESS My hand and the seal of said Court hereto affixed, at Windom, Minn., this 18th day of April A. D. 19 27.

M. B. Severson, Clerk

Hats were passed around for each student to add his or her name for the Christmas gift box. We waited expectantly to see whose name we would draw.

It was Christmas, 1925, and we were seated in the college auditorium during assembly.

When the hat came to John, he read the name on his slip of paper with an exclamation of surprise. The person sitting next to him said, "I will exchange names with you." To this, John replied, "No, I quite like the name I have."

Later he said to his companion, "I prayed that if I drew Viola Bergthold's name, I would propose to her before Christmas."

He did and I accepted.

In the dormitory reception room till "lights out" at 10 o'clock on week-ends

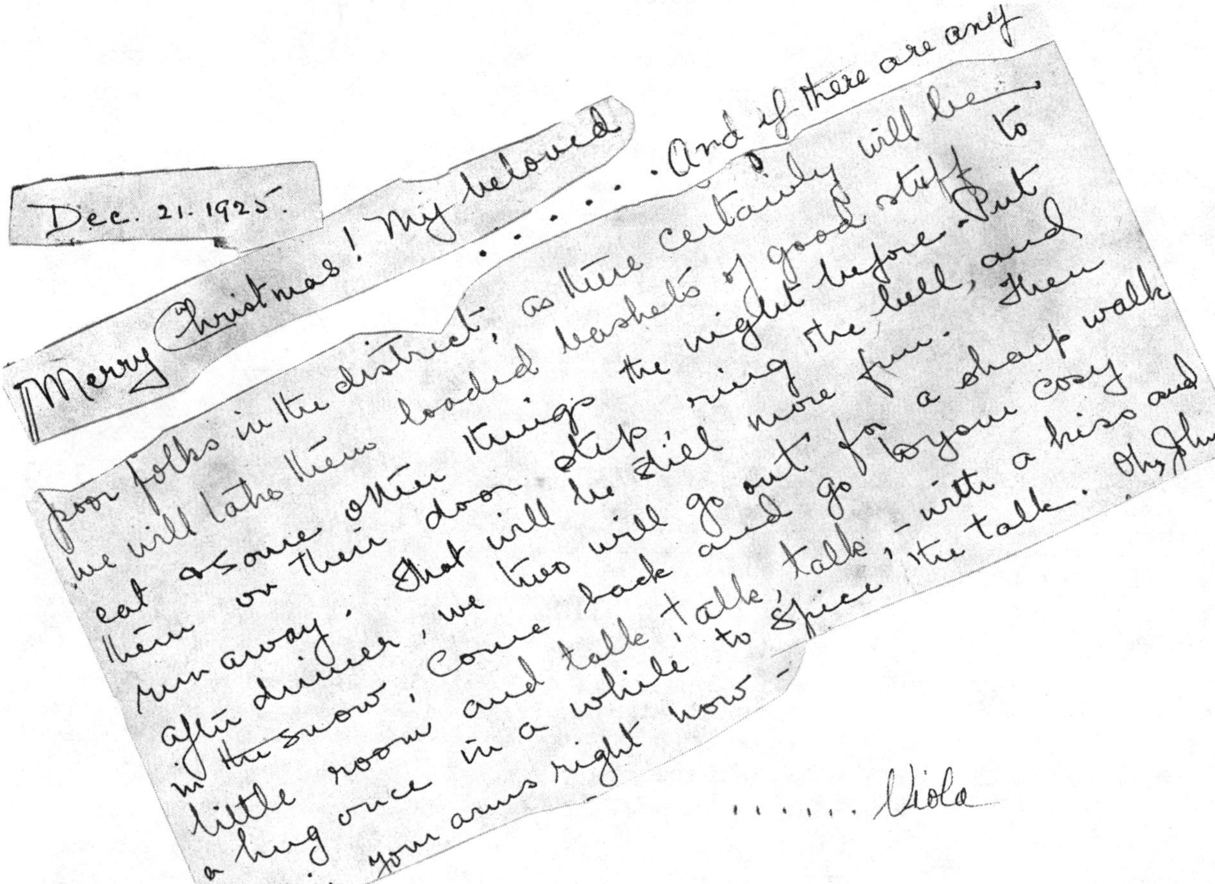

Dec. 21, 1925.

Merry Christmas! My beloved ...... And if there are any poor folks in the district, as there certainly will be, we will take them loaded baskets of good stuff to eat & some other things the night before. Put them on their door step, ring the bell, and run away. That will be still more fun. Then after dinner, we two will go out for a sharp walk in the snow. Come back and go to your cosy little room and talk, talk, talk, — with a kiss and a hug once in a while to spice the talk. Oh, John, to be in your arms right now —

...... Viola

1925

Tabor College
Hillsboro, Kansas

J. A. Wiebe
Blessed is the influence of one true loving human soul on another.

The Class of nineteen hundred twenty-five Tabor College Graduating Exercises May twenty-second College Auditorium ..., Kansas

1926

Memorizing the dramatic declamation of *Queen Esther* took many hours of rehearsing with my teacher Pauline Harms, but it earned me a diploma in Elocution.

Along with forty-eight others in 1926, I graduated from Tabor College majoring in Chemistry, Biology and Bible.

I worked my way through college, washing pots and pans and helping as part-time librarian. In summer I painted dorm floors, or worked in doctors' offices, taking blood pressures and blood specimens.

When my grandfather, Peter Mandtler, died in Canada, he left me my Mother's share of her inheritance of $1000 which helped towards paying my college fees.

In the 1920s, I had very little money to spend on clothing. My wardrobe consisted of two skirts – one a pleated one which John liked, several middy-type blouses and one or two Sunday dresses.

Esther Ebel, a professor's wife, and my lifelong friend, helped me make the dress I wore at our wedding reception. My wedding dress of white satin was made by my Aunt Zella Bergthold, a seamstress who lived in Arkansas, and who, with my Uncle Henry, attended our wedding, representing my parents who were in India.

The above picture was taken while shopping in Wichita, Kansas, with John's sister, Martha, for my $40 wedding outfit. I also purchased a black toque (brimless hat) which I thought was quite daring and becoming.

Later, when John and I were traveling with an evangelist, I wore my toque. The minister gave me a withering glance and said, "You as a prospective missionary should wear a hat with a brim!"

So much for my black toque.

My toque   Hats of the day with brims

Will, lover, this letter must get off to-day. So good bye for this time. I hope to spend long seasons with you this Christmas while in Cond—

With a 'love as strong as death' — as you said — as I say too —

I am yours for always —

all times   X Viola X

January 16, '26
Before daylight

My Beloved Viola, Love's girl.

[...] Can you [...] bed at night? and I have [...] tomorrow [...]

Dear Girl :—

I would like some words with you very soon. I can't stand this any longer.

These last two days have been — Oh! so long and — Please. Still the intense love, John

Viola, I love you, my precious Girl
With that same love
John

Excerpts from Dr. H.W. Lohrenz's letter written 10 October 1925 to my parents in India:

"Es ist vor Eurer Abfahrt, als Ihr die Tochter teilweise meiner Aufsicht anvertrautet... Wie es nun mit Viola geworden ist, ist Euch jedenfalls allseitig bekannt; denn ich habe beiden eindringlich geraten, nichts ohne Euer Wissen und Eure Zustimmung zu tun. Sie haben mir auch beide mitgeteilt, dasz sie dieses getan haben und ich bin unter dem Eindruck, dasz alles richtig eingeleitet und die Entscheidung Eurer Tochter Eure Zustimmung hat. Es ware daher nicht notwendig, dasz ich weiter etwas sage."

"I would like to say that the young man (John) is one of the best of young men we have ever had in our school. He is healthy, spiritual and intelligent. He has a good reputation in his home church as well as among the students and has, through his clean living, shown who he is. I can congratulate you wholeheartedly on your good fortune which the Lord has granted your daughter in getting brother Wiebe as a son-in-law. I believe, as both Viola and John have told me, that they have your blessing... If Viola were my daughter, I could wish nothing better for her and trust her decision meets with your approval... We would like to arrange and pay for the wedding reception and the celebration in your stead... May the Lord bless you and your children."

"With brotherly greetings,"
sd-H.W. Lohrenz

Dr. and Mrs. H.W. Lohrenz and children

The honor of your presence is requested at the marriage of *Viola* daughter of Rev. and Mrs. D. F. Bergthold to *John A. Wiebe* on Tuesday evening, June the first one thousand nine hundred twenty-six at seven o'clock at the M. B. Church, Hillsboro, Kans.

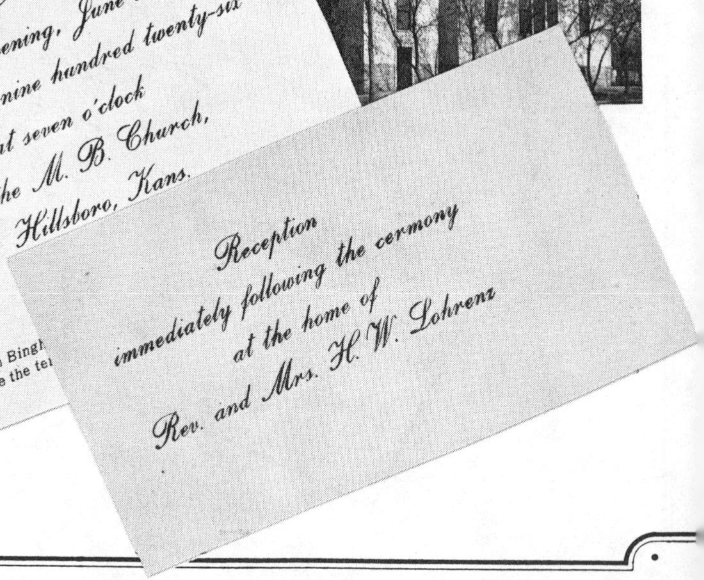

Reception immediately following the cermony at the home of Rev. and Mrs. H. W. Lohrenz

Holy Matrimony

That on the First day of June in the year of our Lord Nineteen Hundred Twenty Six At Hillsboro, Kansas Mr. John A. Wiebe of Bingham Lake, Minn. and Miss Viola C. Bergthold of India – Hillsboro, Kansas, U.S.A.

On a hot, sultry evening, 1 June 1926, John and I were married. Rev. H.W. Lohrenz preached from the Gospel of St. John, Chapter 21, emphasizing three points: LOVEST thou me; Lovest THOU me and Lovest thou ME. My sister Lydia and a friend, Anna Harms, were bridesmaids.

I wore a simple, middy-length white satin dress. Contrary to the mores of the Mennonite Brethren Church, I was the first to wear a veil and carry a bouquet of flowers given to me by John. Rings, however, were not exchanged during the ceremony but John later gave me a gold band.

My uncle and aunt from Arkansas City represented Mama and Papa. John's parents came from Minnesota.

The biggest disappointment of the day was that the garden reception had to be moved to the bleak college cafeteria because of rain. However, we still enjoyed fourteen handmade angel food cakes made by the president's wife, Mrs. H.W. Lohrenz.

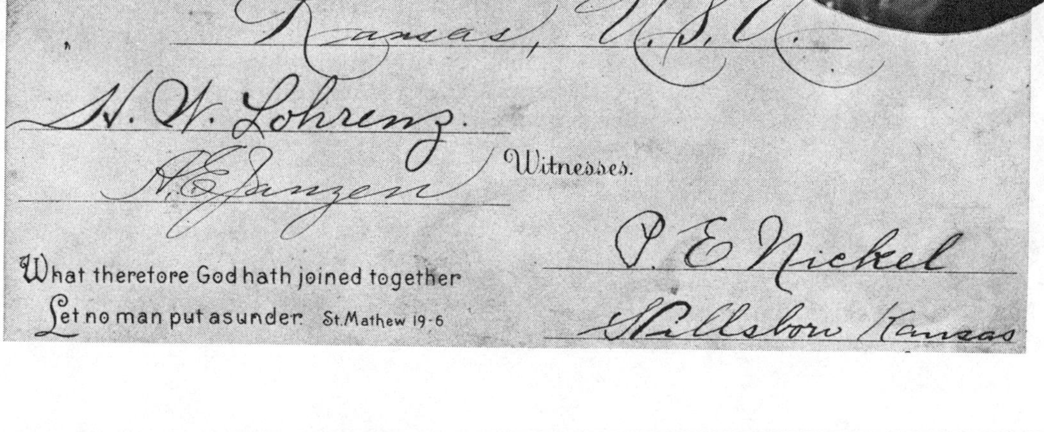

H.W. Lohrenz
H.E. Janzen Witnesses.

P.E. Nickel
Hillsboro, Kansas

What therefore God hath joined together Let no man put asunder. St. Mathew 19-6

The day after our wedding in Hillsboro, Kansas, John purchased a Model T Ford with $400 he had saved teaching in South Dakota. We packed our new car with our belongings and wedding gifts and headed for Minnesota.

On our arrival, Mother and Father Wiebe held a reception for us to meet John's relatives. So as not to offend my in-laws and the church elders, I wore my black dress at the reception as my Mother had done at her wedding twenty-five years earlier "befitting the missionary status."

The Wiebe family was a hardworking, sincere, jovial, closely-knit one into which I was readily accepted.

We spent the summer of 1926 helping John's sister Marie and her husband, Isaac Voth, harvest their crops in Manitoba, Canada.

After the harvest, with a little cash in our pockets, we set out to get acquainted with our church constituency on the west coast and to make ourselves known as their representatives to the mission field in India.

Na tho ra ("Come with me") were the first words John learned in Telugu. I taught him the few words I remembered as we traveled from Minnesota to California, Oregon, British Columbia and Saskatchewan, Canada, over the Rockies and back again.

At times we slept in the car and ate oranges purchased along the roadside. Other times, kind folks shared their food and lodging with us when we reached the areas where we were to speak.

I didn't sleep well unless some window or door was open for fresh air. In one stuffy room, my young husband gallantly tried to remedy the situation by opening the window in the dark. Immediately, I felt the cool air and slept well.

In the morning, we had a good laugh when we noticed that John had opened the closet door.

We had very little cash while traveling and returned to Minnesota with thirty-five cents in John's pocket.

During a quarterly church meeting, John was ordained and both of us were commissioned as missionaries for India by Dr. H.W. Lohrenz, Rev. A.J. Wiebe (father), and Rev. J.H. Pankratz (missionary to India).

In September of 1927, with our trunks and suitcases packed, we headed for Quebec, Canada by train. Time and distance were to separate us from John's parents, but the excitement of returning "home" and seeing my parents after six years softened the pain of parting.

John and I never forgot the words of the ticket collector when he heard we were going to India as missionaries: "To whom much is given, much will be required; the Lord has placed upon you great responsibilities, young people, there is no greater work than teaching about His Love."

Sailing on the *S.S. Empress* of Scotland, 25,000 tons, the largest ship on the Canadian route from Canada to Europe, we met many interesting people. Among them was the British Prime Minister, Chamberlain.

To our dismay, on arrival in London, we found out that the Mission Board in America had not made the proper arrangements for our onward journey from London to India. Our only alternative was to take a cross-country trip down the Rhine River to Marseille, France and board a British liner. This might have been an interesting trip but we had very little money. After days of not eating regularly, we boarded the ship and enjoyed the full course meals which included India's savory curries and delicious tropical fruit.

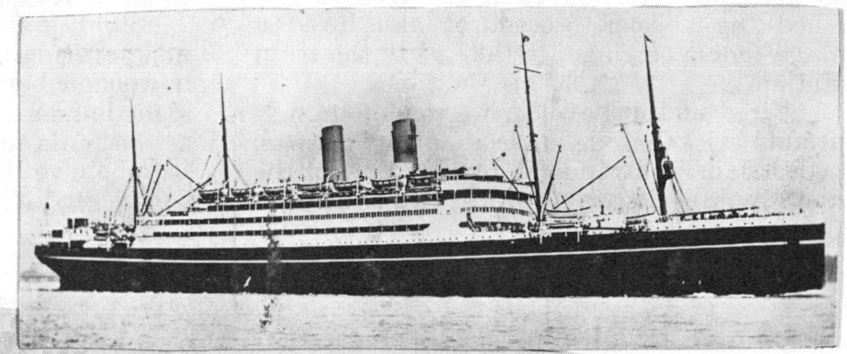

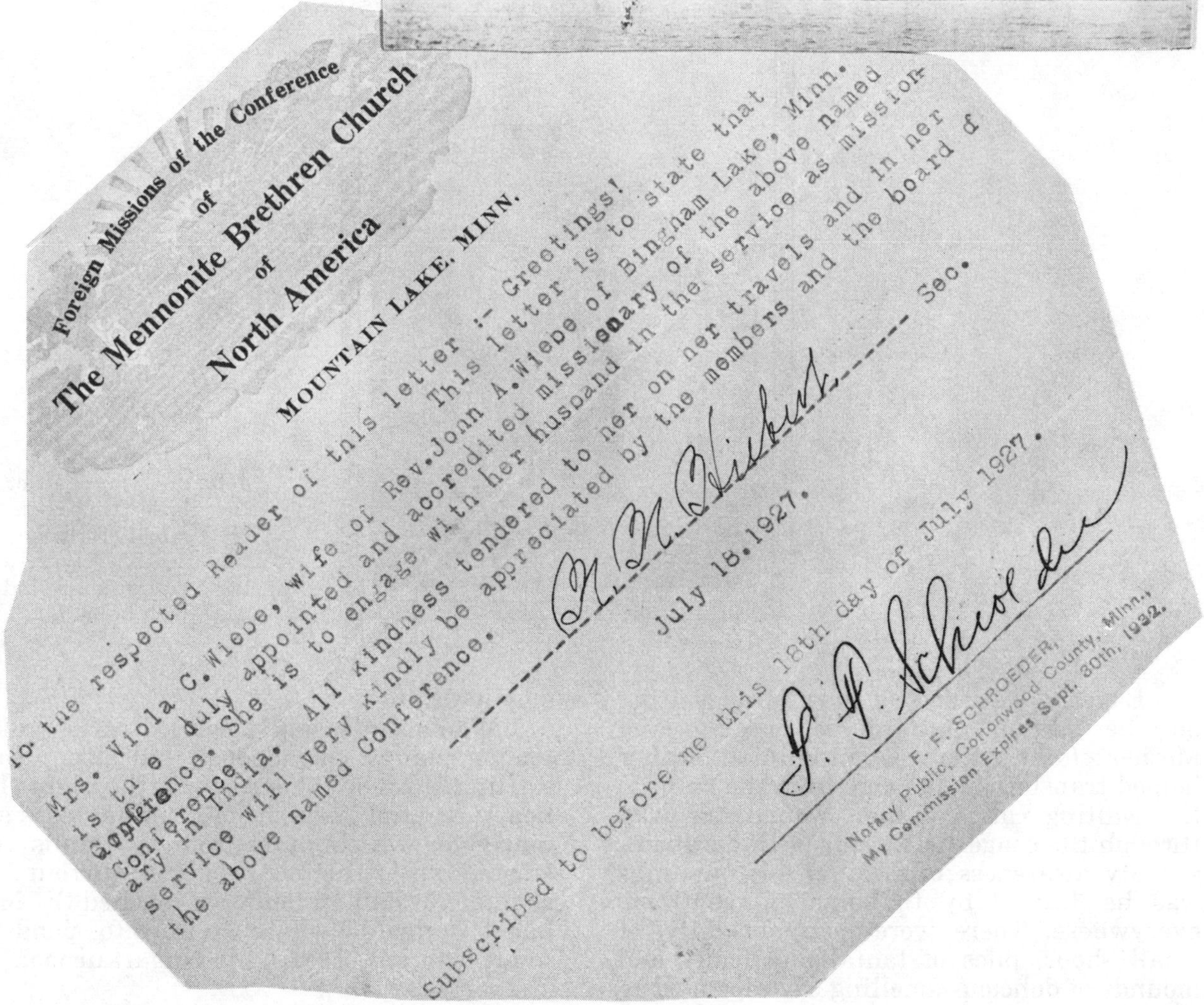

Foreign Missions of the Conference
of
The Mennonite Brethren Church
of
North America
MOUNTAIN LAKE, MINN.

To the respected Reader of this letter :- Greetings!

This letter is to state that Mrs. Viola C. Wiebe, wife of Rev. John A. Wiebe of Bingham Lake, Minn. is the duly appointed and accredited missionary of the above named Conference. She is to engage with her husband in the service as missionary in India. All kindness tendered to her on her travels and in her service will very kindly be appreciated by the members and the board of the above named Conference.

P. N. Hiebert ------ Sec.

July 18.1927.

Subscribed to before me this 18th day of July 1927.

P. F. Schroeder

F. F. SCHROEDER,
Notary Public, Cottonwood County, Minn.
My Commission Expires Sept. 30th, 1932.

Landing in Bombay, we were besieged by sweating *coolies* (porters) wanting to carry our belongings to the port authorities. Steamy heat and a crescendo of excitement and noise engulfed us.

The greater part of the day was spent in various customs offices which one could enter only after presenting the proper documents and *bakshish* (tips). The confusion of the day, including hearing several different languages spoken, was overpowering. Finally, we finished the various procedures and hired a *tonga* (horse carriage) to take us to the train station.

Tired and disheveled, we made our way around rickshaws, lorries, taxis, oxcarts, pedestrians and vendors, forming part of the mass making its way towards the train that was to take us to Hyderabad.

The congestion didn't stop after entering the third class compartment. "To seat forty-five" was written on the side of the carriage. Many more people than that crowded in. Pushing, pressing, women with wailing babies, men cramming tin trunks and bedrolls under seats and on top of luggage racks. Beggars, some with running sores and others imploring with sightless eyes, jostled each other to get to our sides for a *paisa* (coin).

John preferred to sit on a suitcase in the aisle overnight than to crowd with others on a wooden bench. After settling down, John sighed and said to me, "Viola, you tried to describe India to me, but one has to experience it to believe it."

John met my Father for the first time at the Hyderabad railway station in 1927. Both wore light cotton suits and topees (pith helmets).

Eagerly, we searched the crowds waiting on the station platform for Father and Mother's faces. After a joyful reunion, Father helped transfer our luggage from the train to the waiting car. We then wound our way through the congested streets of Hyderabad.

My awareness of familiar surroundings was heightened by the amazing contrasts everywhere. There were many brightly lit small shops, piles of tantalizing fruits and mounds of delicious smelling savories next to smelly drains.

Women in brightly colored saris walked among mangy pariah dogs and sleepy cows settling down on the streets for the night. The heavy scent of garlands of jasmine, roses and marigolds which hung from the stalls contrasted with the odor of the surrounding squalor. In half an hour, we reached the Malkapet Bungalow where we were to spend the night before proceeding to Nagarkurnool.

We slept in an Indian-style tape bed covered with a sheet that first hot night. A mosquito net hung over four wooden posts to protect us from night insects.

At midnight, I was awakened to hear strange noises at the foot of the bed and saw John clawing at the mosquito net, tearing and shredding it from top to bottom.

Hearing the commotion, Mama rushed in, but by this time, John awoke from his nightmare and we were all able to laugh together.

For years to come, I awoke at the slightest noise, fearing John might sleepwalk, especially on the flat rooftop bungalows where we often slept when it was too warm to sleep inside.

After half a day's drive on the dusty roads from the city to the outlying station, Nagarkurnool, we reached our destination. Father and John had to change the tires of the car three times, always surrounded by spectators from the villages.

The mission station my parents had started in 1908, now built up to include a church building, hospital, boarding school for boys and girls, and quarters for teachers and workers, was eighty miles from Hyderabad.

School children who had waited an hour for our arrival lined the path from the gate to the bungalow. Singing "Happy Greetings," they garlanded us with heavy strands of marigolds.

Children crowded around us eager to get a closer look; especially at me, who only a few years earlier had played with their older sisters.

Later in the day, the inevitable welcome program with many speeches, prayers and songs evoked a short response from me in Telugu.

The audience responded with much clapping and smiles when John said, "*Maku tsaala santhoshamu. Vandanamulu* (We are very happy. Thank you.)."

నేను తెలుగు చదువుచున్నాను
= "nēnu telugu tzaduvuzunānu"
= I telugu reading am

Note sentence structure

While living with my parents, John and I studied Telugu with a *munshi* (language teacher). This tutor had no teeth. When he demonstrated sounds, he said, "Watch my tongue, you put it behind your teeth like dish." He was a dear, kind old gentleman and was very patient with us.

We were required to spend the first year learning to read and write, then to take the first Telugu exam given by a qualified committee comprised of *munshis* and missionaries who had passed their third year exams.

John practiced the stories he learned in class with the villagers when he accompanied Father. I increased my vocabulary conversing with the patients in the hospital and the servants in the kitchen. Having grown up in India, sentence structure and pronunciation naturally came easier to me than to John.

Villagers were polite enough not to laugh openly about mistakes Missionaries made while studying Telugu.

— At one conference, the audience was amused to hear the missionary insist that "There must not be 'diarrhea' (*beydulu*) in your midst." His subject was to have been, "There must not be 'differences' (*beydamulu*) in your midst."

— The preachers were not flattered when the "pigs" (*pandulu*) were called to assemble rather than the "preachers" (*pantulu*). A difference of one letter!

JCW

— A servant waiting on the dinner was asked to bring "bed" (*mansamu*). Going upstairs, he brought down a folding camp cot, whereupon the missionary realized he should have said "meat" (*maamsamu*). Just a small inflection made the difference.

— And how must the wife (*bhaarya*) have felt when her husband asked, "Where is my buffalo cow" (*burre*)!

— It wasn't always the missionaries that made amusing statements. We were on the hills one summer when we received a letter from a preacher who mourned the death of his wife. His interesting comment was, "The hand that rocked the cradle kicked the bucket and has left me with six stomachs around my neck."

— The Christmas story took on a new dimension when the children were told that the wise men came on "urine" (*onteelu*). Of course, the preacher had meant "camels" (*ontellu*).

We had been in India just three weeks when a runner arrived from Wanaparty, a mission station about thirty-eight miles to the southwest. He brought word that Rev. Frank Janzen was critically ill and that Mrs. Janzen had taken him to Hyderabad for medical attention.

After committing Brother Janzen and ourselves into the Lord's protection, we hurried to Hyderabad only to hear that our co-worker had died en route to the city.

Foul play was suspected. The police wanted a postmortem done so funeral services were delayed a day. The postmortem, however, proved futile and it was suspected that bribery had influenced the examiners.

Though the tragic story was slow in unravelling, we learned that Mrs. Janzen's compounder, the man who mixed and dispensed medicine, had been dismissed by Mr. Janzen after harsh words regarding the compounder's dishonest practices. Angry at his dismissal, the compounder left the work and started his own practice in the town of Wanaparty.

Months later, the Janzens' cook admitted that the compounder had given him poison to put into the *dora's* (master's) food.

No further action was ever taken.

Mrs. Elizabeth Janzen (wearing a watch chain around her neck), third from the right, at her farewell meeting

Rev. and Mrs. Frank Janzen behind the wicker table to the right, with others at a tea party

The Wanaparty Raja (King) insisted on helping Mr. Janzen build a "suitable" house. Not only was it palatial, but the inside walls were coated with lime mixed with thousands of egg whites to make a smooth shiny finish similar to the palace walls where the Raja lived.

John had been assigned to Wanaparty immediately after language training was finished, but after Mr. Janzen's untimely death, we were told to proceed directly to that mission.

Not without apprehension, we drove to Wanaparty. Mrs. Janzen stood outside the bungalow to welcome us. After sharing a late lunch with her, we began to sort, pack and sell her possessions.

The bungalow was enormous and we needed furnishings so we purchased some of her beds and tables, paying cash for the furniture with money borrowed from our parents because we had not yet received our salaries. For six months we waited for our money. Finally John wrote to the mission board reminding them that we had been in the field for half a year and were living off of borrowed money. Only then did we receive an apologetic letter saying, "Sorry we forgot," and a check for $600.

After this picture was taken of the crown-princess, his brother and sister, the Raja of the Wanaparty Samastan, allowed us to try on the golden bejewelled crowns, and to sit briefly on the throne.

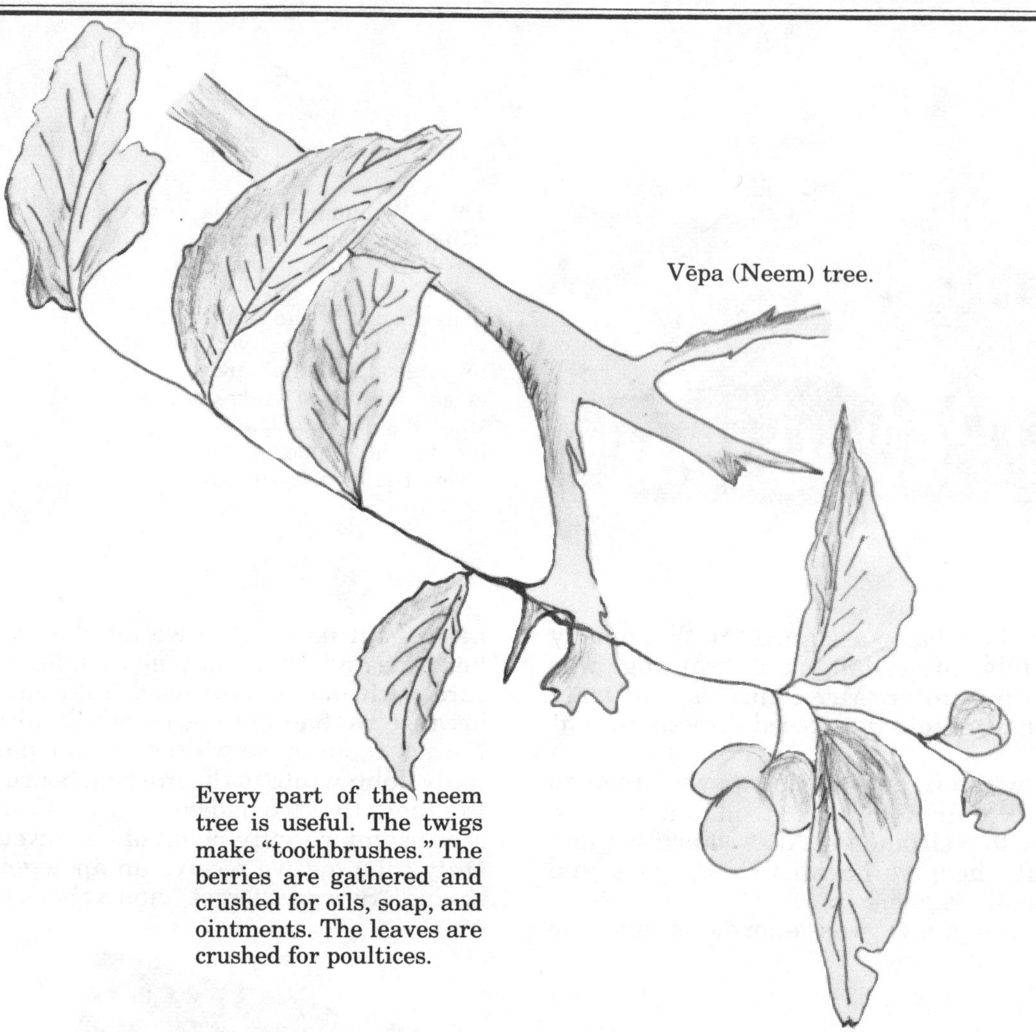

Vēpa (Neem) tree.

Every part of the neem tree is useful. The twigs make "toothbrushes." The berries are gathered and crushed for oils, soap, and ointments. The leaves are crushed for poultices.

During World War I and World War II, quinine was scarce. Mama dried the bark of the Cinchona tree and ground this into powder to give in place of quinine for malaria fevers.

For tick bites, to which some were very allergic, a poultice of the Tangardi leaves (wild shrub bearing yellow blossoms) was made in a mortar and applied to the swollen part of the body. This soon allayed the burning and itching.

Mother made a tonic from cammomile leaves and flowers, and a parsley tea to induce sleep. Cumin, coriander, cardamom and cloves were used as breath fresheners.

In April, 1928, John and I went to the hills of Ootacamund to take our first Telugu exams which we passed with good results.

As our firstborn was due in July, we delayed our return to the plains. On 5 July, our daughter, Esther Eunice was born in Grace Cottage with Dr. Paton and Miss McGill in attendance. Dr. Paton later became the private physician to Queen Elizabeth.

Having purchased a Model T Ford with a gift of money from a friend, Rev. Adams, we traveled down from the hills to Nagarkurnool with our three-week old daughter.

A few weeks later, our parents left on furlough to America leaving John and me in charge of the many facets of work in Nagarkurnool.

No sooner had our parents' car left the compound, when a woman came shouting, "Amma, come, Ballamma is having a baby." I changed my dress and ran to do what I could. Fortunately, it was a normal birth and mother and child did well.

Mama left me much information for mixing various ointments, lotions and cough mixtures from local herbs and other available ingredients. Medicines were not always available and pharmacies were far away. Ramakka, formerly an illiterate village woman, learned much from Mama and could be trusted to take care of any patients and the hospital when John and I were absent.

When weather permitted, we went into the villages, set up camp and held meetings in the surrounding villages.

One afternoon, a young man came limping to the tent and showed us his infected swollen foot and begged us to do something to relieve the pain. He had been to the village "doctors" but the foot had only gotten worse. While I put hot compresses on the foot, John sterilized his pocketknife over a flame and then jabbed it into the festering foot. The pus and putrid matter spurted out along with a large thorn. I cleaned the foot, put on sulpha powder and bandaged it. The relief on the boy's face and his gratitude was evident in his big smile. He bent down and touched our feet, "For haven't you touched mine?"

Actual size of thorn removed

The annual retreat to the hills was both a necessary change as well as an old missionary custom.

The extreme heat of the plains during the summer months was debilitating and the climate in the hills 7000 feet above sea level offered respite and a time for introspection and social gatherings with other missionaries and foreigners.

"Missionary Rest Houses" were often managed by retired missionaries or personnel who came from America specifically for this purpose. Rooms with a bath attached were available for a small price. Meals were catered in a common dining room.

Summer 1930 I spent with Esther in Ootacamund awaiting the birth of our second child.

July 24. 1930

My dearest Beloved One

I've had to cry out of sheer tiredness and lonesomeness to-night. Esther wasn't asleep again when the dinner bell rang, so I left her half asleep & ate my soup, but when I heard her cry, I went back to the room. Miss Hughes has given me to understand that it's a lot of extra work & nuisance to send in trays, so I'd rather starve than be a nuisance. So I'm not having any supper. How I wish these days were over & I could be with you again, where I feel wanted. Never again will I stay in a place called "Missionary Rest House" with the extra sign attached "Children not wanted". I hoped it would be different. But we won't grumble. I'm sure the Lord wants it this way too.

Are you thinking about announcement cards?

Yours with all love, Viola.

Nagarkurnool, July 14 — Wish it was more! Sweet Viola & Baby Esther! How can I stand 20 days more? How can I? It is very hard for me as I miss you so.

Postal Telegraph

VIA RCA
1930 OTACAMUND 20 1207
BERGETHOLD
BAYLOR HOSPITAL DALLASTEX
JOHN CLEMENT ARRIVED WRITE WIEBE
JOHN.

It was my twenty-seventh birthday. John joined Esther and me in our rented house on Missionary Hill where we celebrated quietly. Towards evening we went to Selborne Nursing Home to celebrate some more. Before the day ended, John Clement made his debut on August 17th. What a marvelous birthday gift he was!

It was not easy to fill in for other missionaries. We were often told, "This is what the Voths did," and "This is what they would have done." Missionary Voth had a reputation for being stern but generous.

Every Sunday morning, beggars sat along the dirt path leading from the bungalow to the church. Mr. Voth gave a pocketful of coins to the beggars admonishing them not to spend money on *beedis* (cigarettes) or local brew; telling others to go to the hospital and to send him the bill. Those beggars who had not received anything from Rev. Voth before the service, waited the three hours for the *dora* to reappear.

Petty thievery was a common occurrence not only on the compound but also in the villages. Often, just a reprimand or dismissal from employment, if the theft had been major, was the only punishment given. We seldom reported a thief to the police because the miscreant would either be beaten or have to pay a bribe to go free.

Rev. J.J. Dick was invited for a refresher course to Devarakonda. Preachers and Bible women came to the compound once a month in order to have refresher courses, hear Bible readings and receive their meager salaries. Rev. Dick brought a small portable typewriter and put it in the cupboard of his room. A laborer, thinking he could get rich quick, stole the case and went up into the *konda* (hill). Bitterly disappointed after finding just a typewriter instead of coins in the case, the thief told some boys herding cattle to "go and tell the people at the mission that you have found the case that rattles."

At a Mission Conference in Shamshabad J.H. and Maria Lohrenz – far right, back – in charge. Left back row – J.H. Voth, J.N.C. Hiebert with Phyllis, Viola and John Wiebe with baby John, Father D.F. Bergthold. Middle row – Mary Voth, Anna Hiebert with Grace, Margaret Suderman, Mary Wall, Mother Anna Bergthold with Esther, Katharine Schellenberg. Sitting – Ted Voth, Sam Bergthold, Hugo and Tilly Voth, Catherine Reimer.

Catherine Reimer was resented by some missionaries because of her advanced maternity procedures — by placing the newborn baby on the mother's belly, and making the mother walk from the table to her ward. Having endured much criticism, she did not return to India after furlough, and went into children's evangelism.

Ruins of an ancient fortress rose against the sky above the village of Devarakonda (hill of the gods) nestled against the base of a barren, rocky hill. The mission station was about a mile and a half from the village. The panthers and jackals that roamed the hills now and then took cattle or dogs from the villagers.

With our possessions packed on an oxcart and the Model A Ford, we moved to Devarakonda where we were to work the duration of Rev. and Mrs. J.H. Voth's furlough after my parents returned to Nagarkurnool.

Two single missionary women had been in Devarakonda for many years. Miss Helen Warkentin efficiently administered the school and boarding. Miss Mary Wall, together with the compounder and nurse, had a thriving hospital. Miss Warkentin also fostered orphan girls and helped finance those who could not afford school fees.

Miss Warkentin was saddened one Christmas season when she heard from students returning to school that the poor parents of one of her girls had sold their beautiful daughter to the Nizam's harem.

Devarakonda Mission Bungalow

Helen Warkentin climbing the "hill of the gods"

One day, in broad daylight, when women were busy with household chores and children were playing out of doors, an unusually bold panther made its appearance. It roamed about in a distracted sort of way until, finding the screen door of the kitchen open, wandered in. The terrified cook, seeing his premises occupied by a panther, summoned a policeman from the village who shot the defenseless creature which really had not done any harm.

There was a small government dispensary in the village of Kalvakurty run by a compounder. Still many people came to me for advice and medical attention.

I had a little medicine such as aspirin, iodine and Epsom salts, a few ointments and some knowledge of local remedies that Mother had taught me so I decided to set up a clinic on the verandah of our newly constructed bungalow.

One sultry afternoon, a wrinkled old woman with a faded *riveka* (blouse) and torn sari came to me from a distant village on an oxcart with her sick son.

He was groaning and incoherent with high fever and a swollen throat. The mother explained that she had cooked greens for their noon meal several days previously. Her son, after swallowing some rice and greens, complained of a pricking sensation in his throat. She thought that perhaps a *tummu mullu* (thorn) from the twigs she had used for fuel, had fallen into the greens. Her son had probably gulped down his food, not noticing the thorn until too late.

"Then my husband will have to take your son to the hospital, for he will need an operation to remove the thorn," I said.

The old woman threw up her arms in alarm and said, "No, either you make him better or I will take him to the village to die." Many, I found, had a greater fear of hospitals than death. Death, at least, they were familiar with.

Faced with a challenge, I prayed for wisdom. If the thorn softened with sour greens, then perhaps lemon juice would soften the thorn. On that supposition, I urged the sick man to sip half a cup of pure lemon juice very slowly. He had finished about half of the lemon when he gave a rasping cough, gagged and out came a large *tummu mullu* — which I have kept to this day.

The man seemed to feel immediate relief, his temperature came down and the swelling in his throat disappeared in a few days.

The family folded their hands in thanks, saying *vandanamulu* and went home saying they were going to worship the God who made their son well.

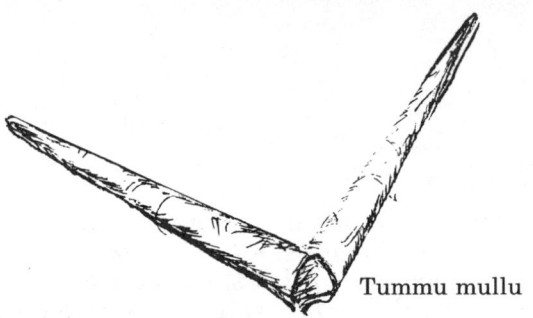

Tummu mullu

Drawing of the thorn removed from the man's throat. The actual thorn is in my collection.

The Voths returned to Devarakonda after their one-year furlough. John and I, together with our children and household goods, moved to Kalvakurty. This was an area delegated to us as pioneer mission work.

We moved into a heavy canvas tent borrowed from our parents. It had an extended flap under which we ate our meals and entertained visitors. The tent was pitched on a slight rise so water could run down the slope when it rained instead of into the tent. A small bamboo structure was constructed for kitchen use and a hole dug for a latrine within an enclosure some distance from the tent.

We quite enjoyed residing in the tent until the monsoon rains started. First the clouds rolled in. Then winds swept over the barren plains swirling dust in and around the tent. Finally, heavy thunder preceeded heavy rains which day after day turned roads into muddy rivulets made worse by tracks from the narrow oxcart wheels. Everything became damp. Mildew grew on all our leather shoes and books. Chairs and tables felt sticky. Clothes hung limply. Spirits also dampened. People sat huddled around small fires built between three stones on which they cooked their meals.

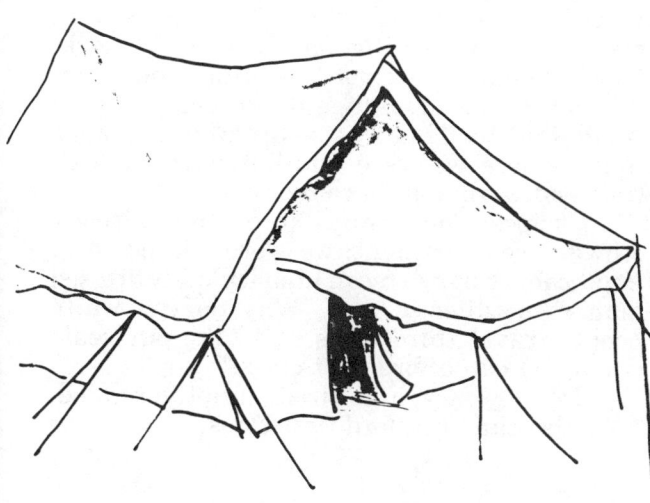

John received sanction from the government to build a mission house and proceeded with the blueprints but finances proved insufficient to start building. Many letters were written to friends and relatives in America telling them of our need. In return, we received some money. We sold our cow and calf for one hundred rupees and added this amount to the building fund.

Stones, which were cut by the *vadari varu* (stonecutters), were brought from nearby hills in *bundis* (carts) for the foundation of the house. Bricks were made on the premises. Preachers and teachers in the area donated hours and hours of their time and labor.

The walls of the bungalow began taking shape into a simple, practical structure. We moved into the building before it was completed.

The floors were spread with cowdung and earth (the usual Indian practice which did not smell after drying but left a smooth dustless surface). Lime was mixed in order to whitewash the walls of the house.

Finally, the window and door frames were put in and the flat roof extended. The bungalow was ready for occupancy and we moved in our few belongings.

The completed Kalvakurty house

The rickshaw pulled by men traversed the rocky slopes

The *khandi,* cloth hammock carried on poles by men

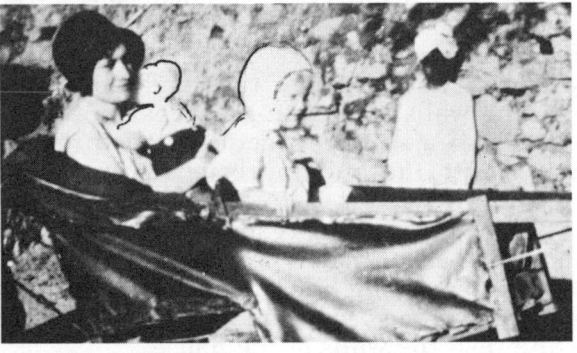

Traveling third class by train, we saved money but the compartment was dirty and crowded. A sympathetic *water walla* (water carrier), seeing our discomfort, invited us to sit with him in the carriage used only to carry earthen pots of water for thirsty travelers. We gratefully accepted. The comparative coolness and quiet was a relief from the stifling, congested compartment. Our two children slept well with the jostle of the train. The journey to the railroad terminal, Dera Dunn, took three days.

Our destination, Landour Hill Station in North India, was not approachable except by foot, horseback or *khandi* (cloth hammock carried on two poles by two or four men). The children and I were carried up the beautiful steep incline in a *khandi*. John preferred to walk.

Our brief retreat in the tourist guest lodge and the cool weather provided a welcome change. *Coolies* (porters) carried the children in large baskets on their backs. John and I hiked behind, watching the *coolies'* strong wiry legs and enjoying the scenic mountains to Mussoorie. Walking beside rushing streams with cold, clear water, winding our way through forests and flower covered meadows, we made our way along well-worn paths, enjoying the crisp air.

Traveling in the north of India in 1931 gave John and me our first exposure to the rumblings of unrest and agitation towards the British Colonial Rule. Now and then we were greeted with hostility or a rude remark. Knowing only a few words of Hindi and Urdu, we had the disadvantage of not being able to communicate. This was so different from the south where we were familiar with the culture and were able to converse fluently.

Pushing our way into the already crowded compartment, we were addressed in impeccable English by an immaculately dressed man in a tailored suit. "Why do you white people travel third class and take our seats when you can afford first class?"

John, weary and tired, quietly replied, "We also cannot afford first class."

We interrupted our train journey back to Hyderabad in the Central Provinces in order to visit other missionaries. In spite of the heat, we toured many projects and enjoyed the interaction with co-workers.

While walking towards a village church one Sunday, we noticed a commotion. Making our way through the excited crowd, we saw a man and a woman in obvious disfavor. The woman had the *pallu* (end of the sari) pulled over her face, the man stood straight but with downcast eyes. We soon learned that the two had been found out to be adulterers. They were now being given the option of being beaten with a shoe in public or to be excommunicated from their church. To be beaten in public was enough of a disgrace, but to be beaten with a shoe was the most demeaning of insults. Even to be touched with a shoe was polluting. If that happened, the offender bent low and touched the other's shoe or foot and said *kshaminzu* (forgive).

The couple chose the public beating and the man lay himself on the step. One of the elders took off his shoe and hit the prostrate man. Two other members of the congregation did the same. We left before any action was taken on the woman.

Another week brought us to the end of our visitation. Bidding farewell to our friends, we boarded another train for the Deccan.

Our travel from one area to another subjected all of us to irregularities and often infection.

The villagers often told me *Neerlu padaledu* (the water was not good at our relative's village and we got sick). This was very likely the case when one considered the pools, stagnant puddles and even some wells from which their water was obtained.

Eye flies, more obvious during the rainy season, were a constant irritation and carried infection from one person to another.

The rains had just begun when we returned to the Deccan. The heat was intense and the eye flies in the unscreened Hyderabad mission bungalow were a menace. We stayed in the otherwise unoccupied Hyderabad bungalow for a few weeks. The former occupants, missionary Lohrenzes, had moved to Shamshabad thirteen miles from the city.

Little Esther developed conjunctivitis, most likely carried by eye flies. Her eyes did not respond to treatment so we took her to the government hospital. Government facilities, at that time, were our only recourse for cases needing hospitalization. Esther's eyes became better in the hospital but she became infected with typhoid fever. Dr. K. Schellenberg, a colleague, advised us how to take care of Esther without having to take her back to the hospital.

After weeks of home nursing and careful diets, Esther regained her strength and cheery spirit and eagerly helped with young brother John.

A five-year old malnourished Susan with two-year old Esther. Susan with much T.L.C. grew bigger fast.

> Joys have been many,
> Sorrows not a few.
> But viewing Heavenly Gifts,
> His Grace,
> It was sufficient unto the hour.
> "THEN, -- Just -- Viola & John
> and now,
> Our Creator's miracle!!
> 'Birdie' Esther Eunice, so nice,
> Johnnie Clement 'Sonnet' so 'sunny',
> "Noni" Viola Ruthie so pretty.
> Tey make our Anniversary so real and happy.
>
> J.A. Wiebe
> June 1, 1933.

Early in the century as various missions realized the necessity of trained nurses to staff the hospitals, most trained school girls in the skills of caring for the ill.

Taking care of lower caste people, carrying bedpans, treating ulcers, making beds and catering to endless trival demands was considered a demeaning task. However, many girls chose this type of training and became excellent nurses sought after by government and private hospitals. Lured by higher salaries, some nurses left the mission hospitals for work in larger cities and towns after they completed the four-year training program.

Nellie, the daughter of a prominent preacher in the Nagarkurnool Field, was sent by her father, Aaran Kelley, to train in the Hanamakonda Hospital. When we looked for a nurse to accompany me to the hills, the hospital staff recommended Nellie. We took her to Ootacamund where she lived with us in Grace House and helped Dr. Anna Degenring at the birth of our third child, Viola Ruth, on 22 April 1932.

Nellie loved the coolness of the hills and slept soundly at night in a room adjoining mine. No bell or call awakened her. We solved the problem by tying a string from her foot to my bed which I tugged to summon her.

John and I returned to the plains in early June with our three small children and Nellie.

John with "Birdie", "Sonnet", and "Noni", on our Chippendale furniture, a gift from our British friends, the Chapmans, in Ooty.

Remedies for Various Ailments

Equal proportions of honey and lemon juice were boiled and bottled. This was a favorite amongst the school children for coughs. Eucalyptus drops on sugar lumps were also effective.

For scorpion stings:
The place where the scorpion had stung was lanced and a few crystals of potassium permanganate and a small amount of potassium bitartrate (cream of tartar) placed on the laceration. Then a drop or two of water which fizzed for a few moments. Then it was wiped off and repeated again. The limb was massaged and an aspirin given orally. The pain soon subsided, provided the patient had come quickly enough after being stung. Otherwise the pain lasted longer.

Earaches were often relieved by cleaning the ears with hydrogen peroxide, then putting in a few drops of mullein oil.

Joint pains often subsided after rubbing eucalyptus oil onto the painful area. The villagers believed strongly in using kerosene for joint pains and also thought that including bat meat in the diet was good for the joints.

Many were plagued with round (and other) worms. For the roundworm, we had a simple remedy which was easily available to the villagers. One handful of pumpkin seeds was roasted, ground and mixed with jaggery (brown coarse sugar) into a ball about the size of a tennis ball. This and only this was eaten throughout the day with as much water as was desired. This had good results within twenty-four hours.

Burn cases were frequent. We had a hard time convincing the relatives of the patients that we had to wash off the dung, mud and sometimes ink which they had used to cover the wounds. The patient, after being washed, was put onto a clean bed and treated with potassium permanganate, weak tea or vaseline, and given an aspirin orally. We gave the patient as much of the following fluid as possible: one liter of water mixed with half a teaspoon of salt, half a teaspoon of soda bicarbonate and two teaspoons of sugar. Then the patient was ordered to rest.

Dill water was most useful for relieving colic. A handful of dill leaves were cooked in a cup of water, strained, sweetened with two teaspoons of sugar, and given (½ to 1 teaspoon per dose) to the colicky child. Pharmacies sold "Gripe Water."

Not only were green papayas good for tenderizing tough meat but the milk which oozed from the green fruit was used for treating indigestion. We stood below the papaya tree and threw sand at the green fruit. The white milk from the bruised fruit was wiped off and used.

The village women did not eat the ripe fruit as they thought it heated the body. Fruits and some vegetables were thought to either "cool" or "heat" the body. Once they realized the nutritional value of the fruit, however, they ate and enjoyed it.

Later, my nurse daughter, Esther, used the pureed skin, seeds and pulp of the papaya as a poultice on large sores, such as bed sores, which healed the wounds better than commercially sold ointment.

Part of a young papaya tree and fruit

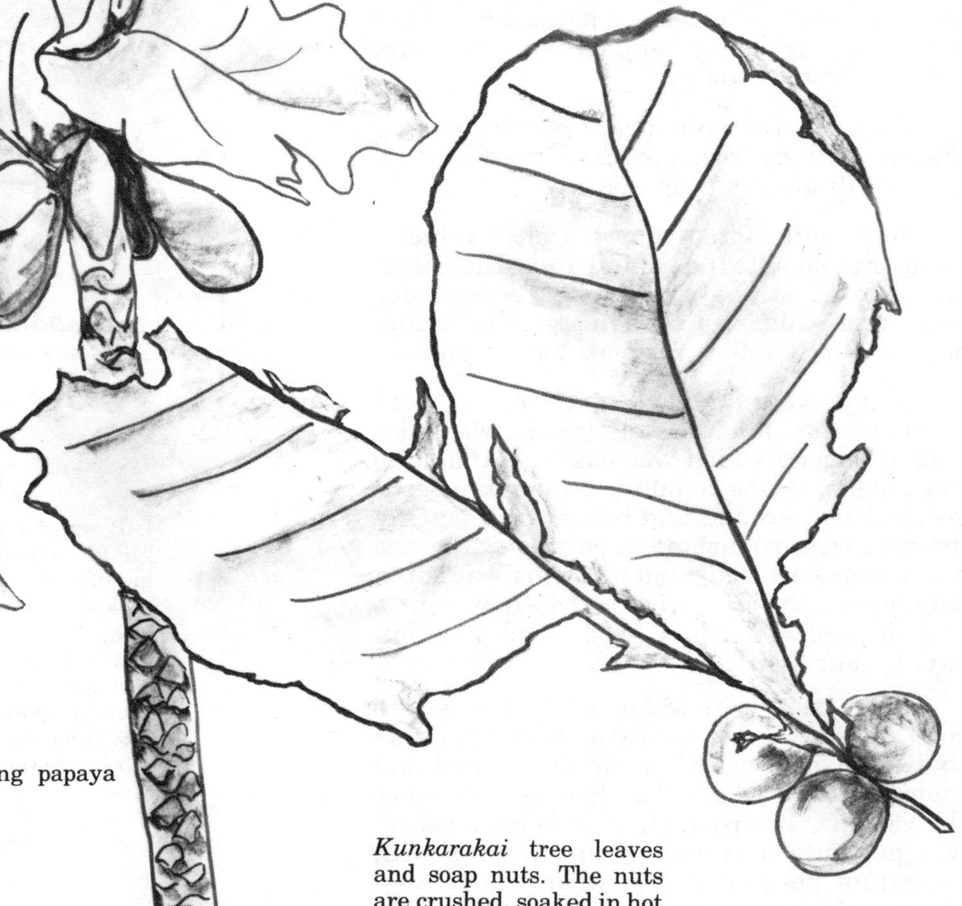

Kunkarakai tree leaves and soap nuts. The nuts are crushed, soaked in hot water, and the suds are used for shampoo.

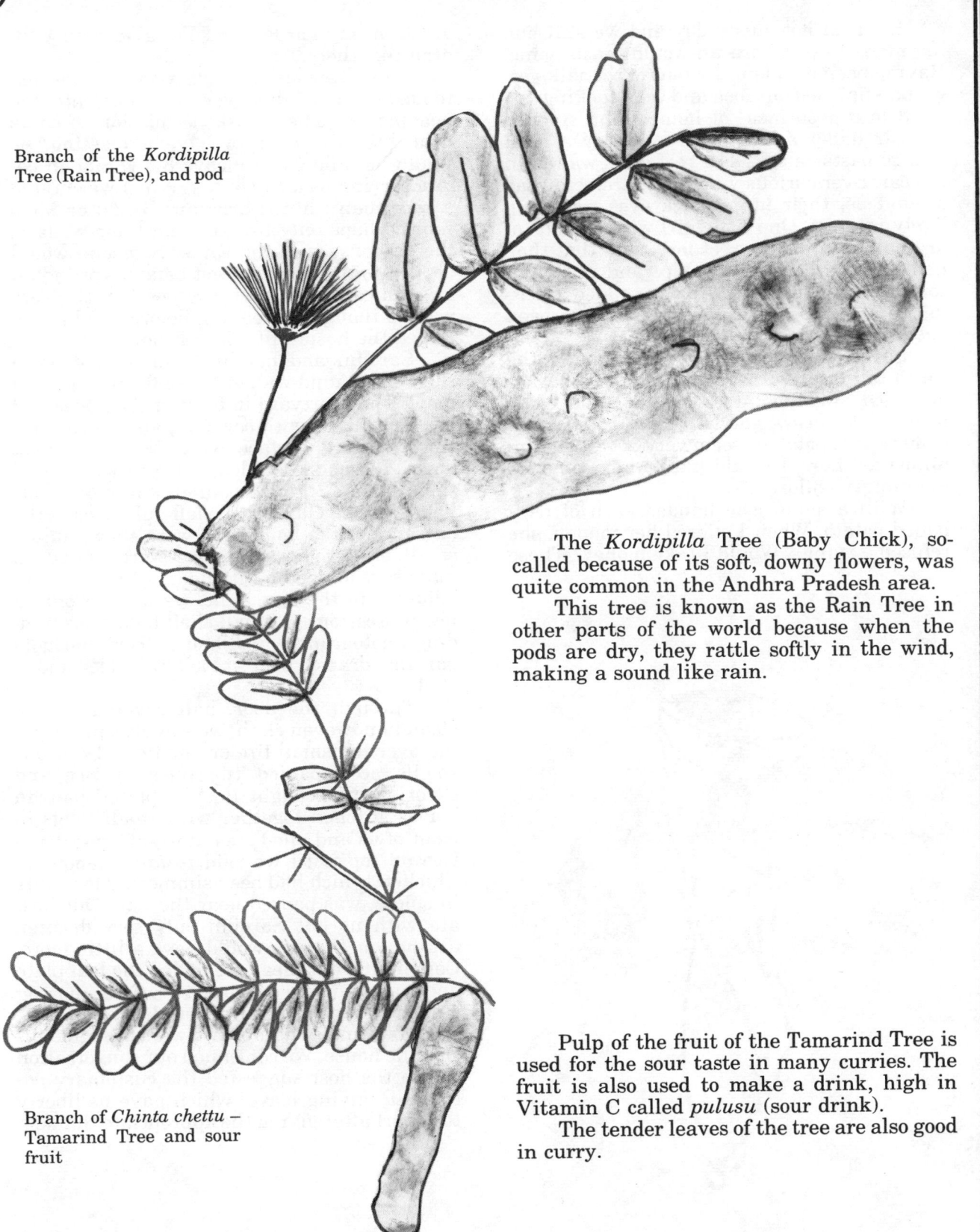

Branch of the *Kordipilla* Tree (Rain Tree), and pod

Branch of *Chinta chettu* – Tamarind Tree and sour fruit

The *Kordipilla* Tree (Baby Chick), so-called because of its soft, downy flowers, was quite common in the Andhra Pradesh area.

This tree is known as the Rain Tree in other parts of the world because when the pods are dry, they rattle softly in the wind, making a sound like rain.

Pulp of the fruit of the Tamarind Tree is used for the sour taste in many curries. The fruit is also used to make a drink, high in Vitamin C called *pulusu* (sour drink).

The tender leaves of the tree are also good in curry.

It was a hot, dusty day and we still had ten more miles before we would reach home. Having been on a lengthy tour of the villages, we had finished our food and were looking forward to a good meal at home. John stopped the car under a banyan tree to pay a local village pastor a call. The rest of us waited in the car. Ever curious village children crowded around us, their large black eyes reflecting lively interest. One little girl with strands of dry hair framing a sweet face, said that they had been gathering cow-chips and rice chaff to mix together for fuel. Another added, pointing to a muddy puddle nearby, "We've been getting water."

Seeing the crowd gathered around the car, a tall, graceful woman carrying a basket of boiled sweet potatoes on her head came nearer. "*Me genzu gaddalu balla bagunnattu* (Your sweet potatoes seem very good)," I complimented her. "I would like to buy some for my hungry children."

With a smile, she handed each of us a boiled potato. When I offered her money, she refused, saying, "Would I take money? These are from my garden and I'm glad your children like them."

This gracious attitude was so often extended to us. Whenever we went into the headman's home to ask permission to camp near his village or to have a meeting, he would not allow us to leave his verandah before serving us a cup of tea. When we entered a poor man's hut, Christian, Hindu or Muslim, perhaps only to ask them their welfare, the response was the same. Someone would be sent to the bazaar to get bananas or Indian sweet-meats or at least *pan* (beetlenut). There was no thought of leaving before one had received the hospitality of that home.

Sarojini and her husband invited us to their small mud-walled house for the evening meal. The courtyard in front of the house had been sprinkled with cowdung and water for a smooth, hard surface which kept the dust down. It was swept clean. Before we entered their home, Sarojini poured water over our hands from a clay jar. We left our shoes at the entrance of the house and were shown into a small dark room where we were seated on mats spread on the dirt floor. After our eyes adjusted to the dim light, we noticed only a few possessions. A small shelf held their wedding photograph which had a dried marigold garland draped over it, a few books and a Bible.

Through the door, half covered with a clean handwoven cloth, we saw Sarojini bending over the small fire on the floor. Delicious smells accompanied the piles of rice and savories she brought in. She placed banyan leaves stitched together with small twigs in front of us and piled steaming saffron-colored rice on top until we said *tsalandi* (enough). Chicken, which had been simmering for hours in spices, was poured near the rice. Our host ate with us but Sarojini only served, often asking whether we would have a little more. Completing our meal, we folded the leaf plate and made our way out to wash before enjoying a fresh banana picked from our hosts' garden.

Mats and a chair or two were brought outside the house. We continued our conversation before the host suggested the customary *povatzunu* (giving leave) which gave us liberty to depart after giving the appropriate thanks.

With her long black braid swinging, Ankamma excitedly ran from the bungalow window where she had been observing the activity inside. Finding Papa and John in a meeting with the preachers, she burst in, announcing to John, "You have a son, I heard him cry."

He hurried back to the bungalow and found me holding Irene Kathryn, a daughter.

Mother and Lydia, my sister who had just arrived to be a missionary in India, assisted with the birth of Irene on 6 November 1933.

We engaged Susanna as *ayah* (nurse) to help me with my four healthy children all under the age of five. Earlier, Susanna had taken care of my youngest brother, Sam, and was a willing, faithful worker and friend.

Christmas 1933

"*Weinacht ist Heut wir sind erfreut* (Christmas is today and we rejoice)." It was four a.m. on Christmas day. Much as I had done as a child, our children now stood at their grandparents' door and sang lustily enough to awaken them from sleep. "It's too early, *kinderlein*," we heard my Father say, "go back to bed." Giggling, the children scampered back to their rooms but certainly not to sleep.

Before dawn, the lanterns were lit and we gathered around the large dining room table to examine the plate each one had put at their place the night before, with the expectation that they would be filled with nuts, sweets, available fruits and a small gift or two.

Father read the beautiful Christmas story before we lifted our voices in praise as we sang familiar carols together. Then Abraham, the cook, *ayah*, gardener and others with their families were called in to come and receive their gifts: shirts and *panchas* (loin cloths) for the men, saris and material for blouses for the women, and clothes and toys for the children.

No one felt hungry for breakfast, but Mother urged us to eat a bowl of *ragi* (millet cereal) knowing we would be hungry before the inevitable three or four hour Christmas program and church service was over.

The school children, with colorful large hair ribbons and jasmine tied to their immaculate coconut oiled plaits, sat restlessly on mats near the front of the church. Their parents and kin, the women with their heads covered with the ends of their saris, sat on benches behind.

This was Children's Day and the stage was theirs as they reinacted the Christmas Story. Lines of shepherds, angels and sheep paraded in front of the delighted audience but a general hush pervaded when Mary, Joseph, the precious child and the wise men took center stage.

After the program, the school children lined up for their Christmas bags filled with puffed rice, brown sugar lumps, peanuts and fruit.

Christmas joy was shared with well-wishers after the program and then we made our way to the bungalow for hot, spicy chicken curry and rice.

The Christmas message was told and a program given in every village occupied by even a small group of Christians. Generally, the entire community attended the event. After the program, pastors usually provided a curry and rice meal for their congregations. Women's groups who had sewed modest garments gave these to the poor and to leprosy patients. Widows were given saris and blouses. Patients in the hospital received gifts of food and were told the Christmas message.

Recollections

"The thirty-mile trip to Nagarkurnool was usually hot, long and dusty, but the prospect of visiting our grandparents was exciting. We took food along and enjoyed eating it at the Traveller's Bungalow.

"Dad stopped in many villages to talk to people. We children often stayed in the car and got very restless and self-conscious because of the curiosity of the villagers who inevitably surrounded us. Once we overheard the village children discussing whether we had arrived for the circus, not realizing that we spoke Telugu. Sometimes we would race to the back of the wheels of the Model A Ford to taste the dust collected on the rims of the tires.

"Grandpa watched through binoculars in anticipation of the small cloud of dust which indicated our car winding down the road. By the time we arrived, our beloved grandparents would be waiting on the front steps of the bungalow. Soon all the compounders and school children gathered around to say *salaam* (greetings).

"Grandma led us into the cool, clean, dark rooms where the smell of cooking permeated the air. The cook usually prepared chicken curry for us.

"Exploring every nook and cranny of Grandpa and Grandma's garden was a special delight. The garden was such a contrast to the hot sand and withered grass — verdantly, refreshingly green. Succulent red and yellow tomatoes hung heavily from their vines. Guinea hens vied for perches in the many fruit trees.

"Dusty, very splendid old-fashioned horse-drawn *tongas* (buggies) stood in the sheds at the far end of the compound. We pestered the drivers to give us rides on the black, leather seats.

"The front porch was shaded from the morning sun by myriads of blue morning glories. When the blooms faded, we sucked the honey from the base of the withered flowers. Small clay pots of parsley, dill and other herbs covered with protective thorns against passing cattle, sat on the corner of the verandah amongst pots of flowers and ferns. Cautiously we picked a leaf or two from the herb pots, crushed them and inhaled the pungent odor or chewed the leaves slowly.

"The kitchen, Abraham the cook's territory, was away from the main bungalow. Hanging from the large *Neem* Tree near the kitchen, was a cheesecloth dripping whey — the makings of cottage cheese for Grandma's famous *verenicke* (cheese dumplings).

"It was fun to visit the press, near the kitchen, and watch the men put letters together, or sew binding on books. Grandpa welcomed cautious curiosity and offered to print our funny little books. He had a darkroom with a red bulb where he developed his own pictures. One day he reached up on a shelf for something and brought down a mother scorpion. We were amazed that he had not been stung.

"Grandpa's huge old rolltop desk with many mysterious little compartments fascinated us. We often hovered around him while he sat at his desk showing us his neat little drawers filled with 'treasures.' He kept garlic on his desk which he chewed for his heart trouble. We loved to play with and comb his white hair and competed for his attention. Once in a while, a mad, wild Telugu woman came to his window and pled and complained to him. Grandpa would continue to work at his desk, occasionally offering comments. The woman would then get tired and wander away. We called her *Pitchamma* (crazy one).

"There were *pomegranate* (tropical fruit) bushes bordering the path to church. If a ripe fruit was found, it was shared and each luscious, brilliant kernel savored.

"Church was very often a very long ordeal. Energetic, rousing singing and long, long sermons. The *Peetra, Pootra* (Doxology) song signaled the end of the service and release. We all heartily joined in.

"Very often we children joined Grandpa on his evening walks. He carried a cane to prod into holes to frighten away snakes. Sometimes we walked to the deep well where large branches of the tree were draped with Oriole nests. We loved to watch the birds dive into the water. Trenches of mud led from where the oxen drew water from the well to the gardens and we longed to play in them but were not allowed to.

"Watching the sun go down between the warm, flat rocks between the garden and the bungalow prompted Grandpa to exclaim at 'Our Creator's works and the beauty of them.' Arriving back at the bungalow from our walk, we would find a fine, linen tablecloth covering the dinner table set on the outside verandah. The centerpiece on the table was generally a beautiful informal arrangement of crimson bouganvilla, taken from a magnificent creeper which splashed color across one end of the shed. Grandma's meals were superb.

"Evening prayers began with the usual scramble to sit at Grandpa's feet as he sat in his wicker chair. Then we heartily sang familiar hymns accompanied by Grandpa's mouth-harp or accordion, followed by scripture and prayers — long, long prayers. Each one prayed, from the youngest to the eldest. Sometimes the youngest fell asleep, or feigned sleep. When we asked Grandpa whether he had said everything in his conversation with God, he chuckled and said, 'I could say much more.'

"Nighttimes spent on the rooftop verandahs were the finest of all. First we looked through Grandpa's telescope pretending to see what we were supposed to be seeing in the clear Indian night sky. Grandpa pointed out various constellations. Then we would crawl under our mosquito nets and lie back to wonder at the heavens and eternity. The starlit sky, the breeze moving gently through the mosquito nets and the penetrating quiet of rural India provided a setting of ineffable contentment.

"A trip to the bungalow bathroom at night was sometimes quite an excursion through real and imaginary dangers. Snakes and scorpions were infrequent but nevertheless seen sometimes. The dimly lit back rooms of the bungalow were haunting, especially when kerosene lamps cast ominous shadows on the high walls.

"The first yawn from Grandpa was the signal for quiet; the second indicated his appreciation of rest and the third ushered his departure to the world of sleep. All of us slept very soon after his familiar, steady snoring."

The above are some recollections of our four oldest children.

Right – The Chippendale suite given us by Mrs. Chapman. It was later made more "valuable" by young son David who carved across the top of the settee with his new penknife!

Below – A visit to the Chapman home in London.

Preparations were made to leave for a one-year furlough to America in 1935. As most of our furniture would be used by others during our absence, we did not have to store chairs and tables. Bedding and other articles which we would use again were packed in boxes and trunks. Knowing that we were leaving, many came to bid farewell and to receive a bundle with some clothing, bottles or other useful items.

Before the doctor would sign our travel documents, we were each required to get a smallpox vaccination given by a government vaccinator.

Several hours after the vaccinations had been given, Irene began running a high temperature and Viola Ruth was having convulsions. I put the girls into a tub of tepid water to reduce their temperatures and then we took them to Devarakonda where Mary Wall, the nurse cum paramedic, further treated them. By now we were sure that the serum had been contaminated.

By the time we boarded the train for Bombay and our departure from India, Esther's vaccination had become severely infected. After boarding the P. and O. Liner, we contacted the ship's physician who told us that if we had waited longer the arm may have had to be amputated.

Esther recovered, as did the others, and we enjoyed the sea, although stormy, and looked forward to visiting the Chapmans in London. They had been wealthy tea planters in North India and came to vacation in Ootacamund where we met them. Mrs. Chapman never forgot John's and my assistance after her husband's death and insisted we visit her.

1936

Our family portrait taken on furlough

OF FOREIGN MISSIONS

Conference of the Mennonite Brethren
Church of North America

Dec...

TO Whom This May Concern:

This ...
Rev. John A. Wi...
and
Mrs. Viola Wieb...

are ordained missionaries of th...
Mennonite Brethren Church of Nort...
they are under appointment to serve in ...
on the mission field near Hyderabad, Deccan, I...
They are authorized to render such service as is
usually associated with the calling of an ordained
missionary.

Very sincerely,

H. W. Lohrenz
Executive Secretary
and Treasurer

Book 3

1936 - 1961

Before we had gone on furlough in 1935, negotiations had been started between the Mennonite Brethren and Baptist Missions about the possibility of turning over Mahbubnagar, Gadwal, Jadcherla and Shadnagar mission stations to the Mennonites. While in Hillsboro, Kansas, John and I had been privileged to present this proposal to the Mennonite Brethren Board of Foreign Missions. They were not only prepared to accept the offer of the Baptist Mission, but also asked us to take responsibility for this area of work.

Our destination in America was Minnesota where John's parents, Rev. and Mrs. A.J. Wiebe lived. We stayed with them for several weeks. We enjoyed fresh produce from their garden and becoming reacquainted with John's relatives. On Sundays, the church constituency was eager to hear reports of the work in India.

Fall and winter months were spent in Dallas, Texas, where John enrolled in the theological seminary to study Hebrew, Greek and other subjects towards a degree in Divinity.

Spending many hours in our van traveling for six weeks, we gave programs in Mennonite Brethren churches the summer of 1936. At every program, our children dressed in different costumes and gave a little speech telling something about the people whom they represented. I wore a sari and told about women and hospital work. John showed slides and challenged the congregations to continue in giving and praying.

The year went very quickly. Particularly as we celebrated Christmas early in order to reach Quebec to be joined by Rev. and Mrs. A.A. Unruh and family for our return journey to India.

We sailed on the *S.S. Empress* of Scotland to Hamburg, Germany, where it is bitterly cold. Because of the Christmas season, we found it difficult to find hotel accommodation. We finally found a cold little room on the seventh floor of a cheap hotel.

While the rest of the family attended children's theater and toured the city, Ruth, who had developed pneumonia, and I stayed in bed in the miserable unheated room trying to keep warm.

The very talkative maid who kept flouncing the pillows to make her point, was amused at us huddling under the covers. She informed us that Hitler was trying to reform those with bad behavior. Men who sexually misbehaved, she said, were castrated. Most of her friends and the hotel personnel were pro-Hitler.

When our ship left Hamburg, we stood at the ship's railings and watched those standing on the pier give the "Heil Hitler" salute.

Our cabins on the *S.S. Bremen* were warm and comfortable. The ship's doctor gave Ruth the necessary medication but scolded us as *verdolte Americaner* (dumb Americans) for giving Ruth ice cream which she asked for and thrived on.

Warmer days followed. Soon we could see the shores of Ceylon on the horizon. We spent a few days there before sailing to Madras where we disembarked.

Above — Viola Ruth between John and me, recuperating from her illness, and Irene.

The A.A. Unruh family and the Wiebe family on rickshaws on the beautiful Island of Ceylon.

Return To India

In 1937, Rev. and Mrs. J.A. Penner invited us to Mahbubnagar and handed over charge of the area along the railway where the Baptist missionaries had been working for over fifty years. We found a well established mission with seventeen acres within the city limits of Mahbubnagar. There was a church, dormitories for boys and girls, housing for employees, and teachers, a building for school purposes and two wells for water.

The fifty-seven acres of land in Jadcherla, ten miles northeast of Mahbubnagar, later became the Medical Center. Dr. and Mrs. J. Friesen and Dr. and Mrs. G. Froese built this thriving hospital where Dr. P.B. Arnold is now the medical superintendent.

Gadwal was located near the Krishna River where the Rev. and Mrs. A. Unruh worked touring in the villages. Margaret Willems and others established the hospital. Shadnagar was the home of Rev. and Mrs. R. David who worked in the area evangelizing in the villages.

The Mahbubnagar Brethren High School of which John was principal, until Dr. D.J. Arthur took over, had an enrollment of 400. The young men and women from the mission area were trained by eighteen teachers. The school was recognized by the government officials who preferred the training their children received in our school. The students excelled in competitive functions with other schools.

John's work as legal advisor for the mission, required much time acquiring documents and papers in the offices of Hyderabad for the purchase of land for church buildings and permits for building. With patience and persistence, he achieved the desired results and became known as the *doragaru* (respected one) who knew and got what he wanted.

The Bungalow

The Mahbubnagar bungalow was built with verandahs on all four sides. The ceilings were high with screened transoms to ventilate the rooms. Outside walls were thick and doors large in order to allow through drafts.

The upstairs two bedrooms were large, high-ceilinged and airy. Each room had a small verandah attached, surrounded by parapets.

The bungalow was our personal domain where upstairs, at least, John and I could find respite from the endless *manavis* (requests). It was too large and prominent, however, in comparison to the other structures on the compound. John often thought that the bungalow should be converted into schoolrooms and that we should build a smaller house.

Many years later, the bungalow was made into a radio studio, then into school offices and the headmaster's residence.

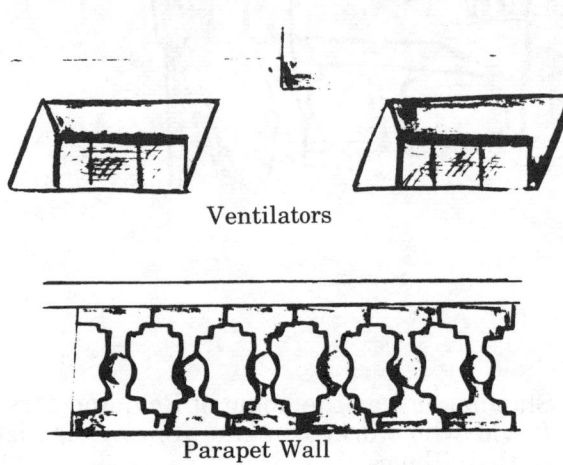

Ventilators

Parapet Wall

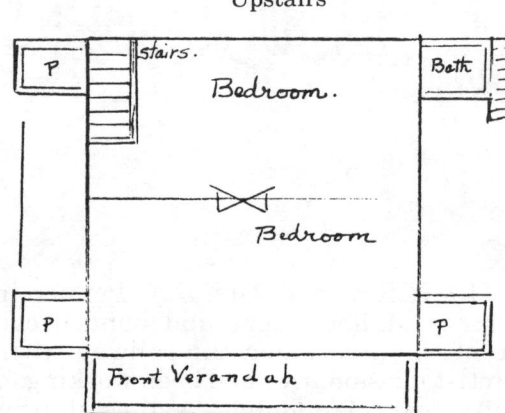

Upstairs

P = open porches.

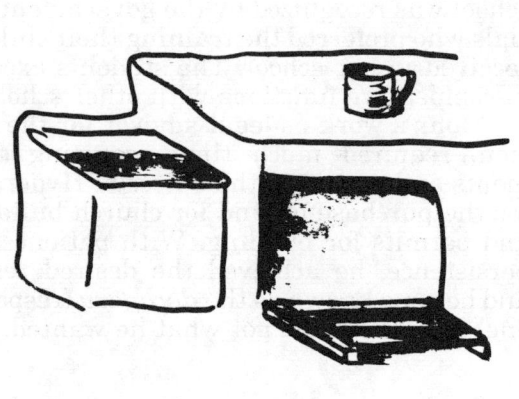

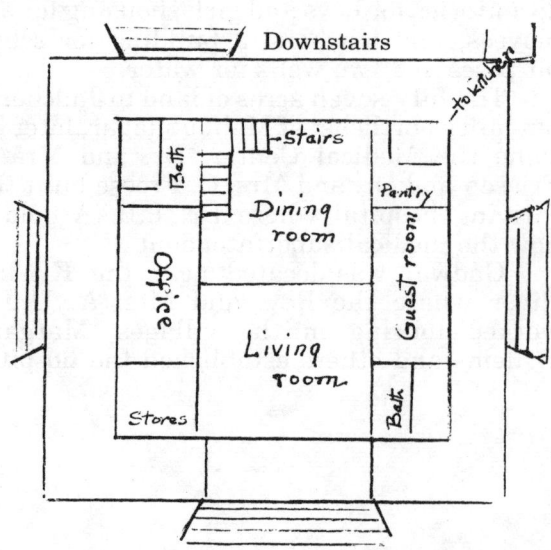

Downstairs

The thirteen acre compound in Mahbubnagar, surrounded by brick walls and two main gates.

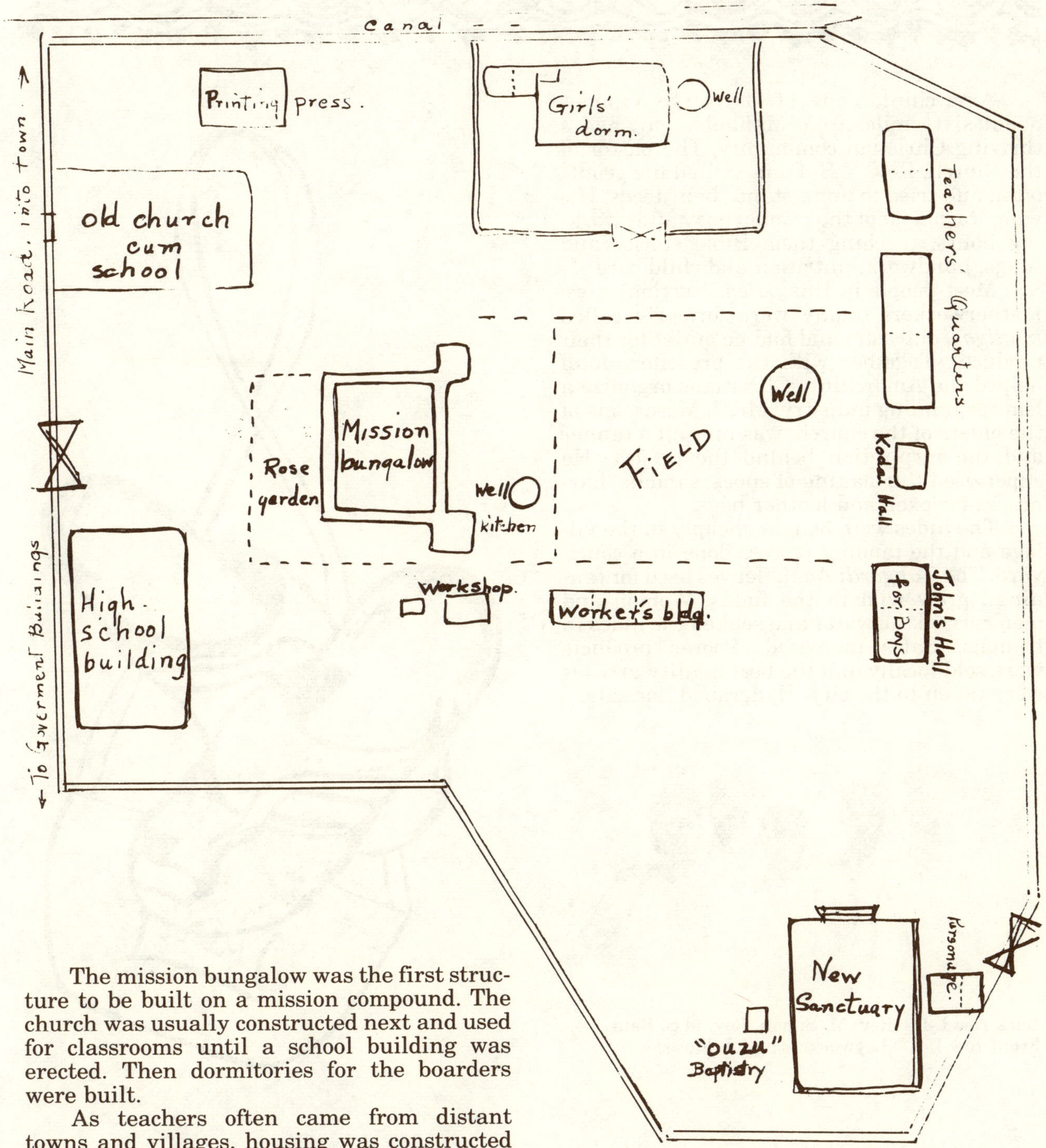

The mission bungalow was the first structure to be built on a mission compound. The church was usually constructed next and used for classrooms until a school building was erected. Then dormitories for the boarders were built.

As teachers often came from distant towns and villages, housing was constructed for them and for the workers such as the cook, *ayah*, cattle herders, school tenders and gardeners.

Amarchinta, one of the large villages about sixty miles from Mahbubnagar, had a thriving Christian community. The pastor of the church, Rev. M.S. Paul, visited his people often and tried to understand their needs. His wife, Rachel, kept the women busy after working hours, teaching them Bible stories and songs, handwork, nutrition and child care.

Most people in this *palem* (section) were leatherworkers (many were formerly called *madigas*, outcaste) and had no outlet for their products. Together with the preacher, John helped the Amarchinta Christians organize a leather tanning industry. Mr. J. Moses, one of the elders of the church, was himself a tanner and the inspiration behind the project. He supervised the making of shoes, sandals, harnesses for oxen and leather bags.

The hides were bought cheaply in the village and the tanning process done in a courtyard. The *Tangardi Aaku* (leaves used for tanning), grew wild in the fields. Women and men carried the water and soaked the hides in troughs. Sales increased. Poorer products were sold locally and the best quality articles were taken to the city, Hyderabad, for sale.

Back row L-R – Rev. M. Simon, Rev. M.S. Paul
Front row L-R – Layworkers and J. Moses

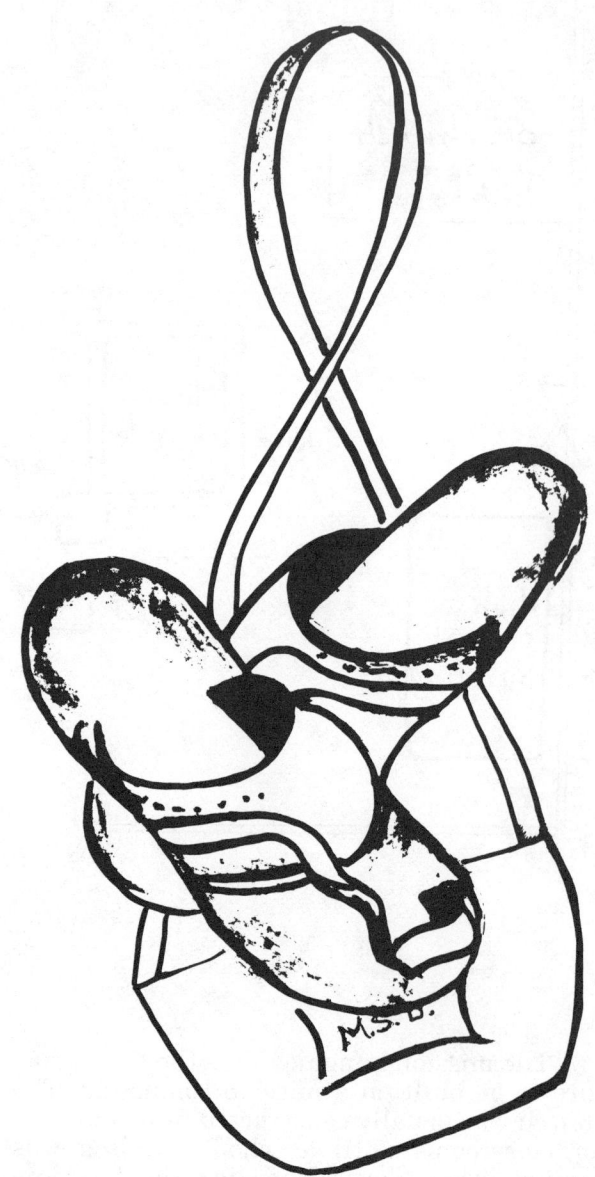

Salaries given by the mission to the church personnel were so meager that John and my father encouraged the preachers and elders to purchase small plots of land and a team of oxen for ploughing. This helped them augment their salaries and become more self-sufficient with food production.

Some who showed skill in carpentry were helped with getting tools, and encouraged to make plows, door and window frames, chairs and tables.

Improved skills provided opportunities to improve living conditions and standards. Many took advantage of opportunities to develop their skills and supplement their incomes.

Women were also encouraged to weave more baskets and mats. We purchased large quantities of mats for the school boarders to sleep on or sit on while studying and eating. Baskets were always needed for sorting and transporting grains and produce. Women improved the family income quite substantially by weaving.

In June of 1937, I traveled with Dr. J.S. and Naomi Carman to Hanamakonda Mission. I was eight months pregnant, and quite edemic. The fetoscope showed two heartbeats so we decided that I needed to be under a doctor's supervision.

As the time of delivery drew near, John drove from Mahbubnagar which was 180 miles to the south to be with me. The afternoon of 20 August, I called John and told him that I would deliver soon. Dr. Carman asked John to hold the chloroform mask over my nose as the doctor waited for the babies to be born.

David arrived first, followed fifteen minutes later by Paul. Paul was quite blue and very quiet, apparently as a result of too much anesthetic. Doctor Carman soon revived him, however. By this time, a nurse had arrived and there was much rejoicing at the birth of twins.

Two weeks later, my parents arrived and we traveled with them to Mahbubnagar. It was quite common in Indian homes for one of a pair of twins to die soon after birth. Often the mother deprived one child from nursing, assuming that she did not have enough milk for two. People were amazed how healthy our twins, David and Paul, were, and realized that they also could breast feed two. We hired Gnanamma, a Bible woman, to help me with the children. This enabled me to return to work.

Kalvakurthy Mission was also under our jurisdiction. While John visited church preachers in the surrounding villages, I dispensed advice and medicine to the sick. The children accompanied us, attended by the *ayah,* Gnanamma. I encouraged her to keep the children away from the sick but often the twins insisted on staying with me.

After one such visit, Paul came down with a severe cough. Despite his illness, we decided to attend the mission conference in Hughestown. While there, Paul's condition deteriorated and we consulted a doctor at King Edward's Memorial Hospital. He informed us that our son had diptheria and would require emergency surgery.

A successful operation was performed and Paul was placed under the supervision of a nurse and me in an isolation ward. After coming out of the anesthetic Paul experienced labored breathing. Anxiously, John summoned the doctor. Dr. Franklin, seeing the state Paul was in, immediately applied oxygen to the tube protruding from Paul's trachea. Our little boy's color was very blue and his pulse very slow. The doctor hastily removed the tube and shouted for an applicator which was not ready, so he dipped a long feather into some solution and put it into the opening of the throat. After the feather was removed, a hard piece of mucas membrane was exposed and the doctor pulled it out. Paul's breathing returned to normal and we breathed a prayer of relief.

Untouchables were considered unclean with undesirable habits such as eating beef and raising pigs. They worked with the hides of animals and most of them we knew were leatherworkers.

They generally lived on the outskirts of villages and had no land of their own, but worked as laborers for their high caste neighbors. Some did tenant farming. They were very poor, treated as inferior, and lacked equal opportunity and leadership.

After purchasing grain or other commodities, the outcaste person dropped his coins on the counter or into the hand of the merchant. Sometimes, these coins were put into a purifying solution to sterilize them. A stick of incense was lit at the doorway of the shop to disinfect those, such as untouchables, who entered the shop.

Occasionally, a high caste person, seeing an untouchable, crossed the street in order to avoid the shadow of an outcaste. In the early days, children of outcastes were not allowed to attend the same schools as caste children. Slowly a few outcaste boys were admitted and allowed to sit at the back of the room or on the verandah outside. While passing a small village school one day, I glanced through the window to see the teacher throwing a clod of dirt at what must have been an unruly outcaste boy at the back of the room. Sticks were not used to punish a miscreant outcaste child because "pollution would pass through the stick."

Conditions changed for the *Madigas* and *Malas* when many of them became Christians. Missionaries started schools for untouchables and caste children; girls as well as boys. Gradually, teachers who were often of the lower caste were brought into the schools.

After the "Portition" in 1947 *Namaste* with hands pressed palm to palm, became the traditional gesture of greeting, instead of *Salaam*.

Mahatma Gandhi called the untouchables *Harijans* or "People of God" and asked that they be given equal rights in society. Gandhi urged those who heeded his words and other freedom fighters simply to refuse by non-violent means to obey the British laws which they considered unfair.

More and more Indians were drawn to Gandhi's words. Thousands were jailed for disobeying their colonial rulers. Crowds followed Gandhi everywhere. One day we were pleased to see him.

John and I were traveling on the train between Guntakal and Madras. The train stopped frequently at stations and we noticed crowds of people throwing little bundles of coins and congregating outside the third class carriage next to the one in which we were traveling.

We got out at one of the stations to look into the window of the carriage and saw a frail man lying on a pad on the wooden third class seat — the much revered Gandhi. In recognition of the people who came to see him and throw coins to him for his work, he bowed his head and folded his hands in thanks.

Bible women's participation was an integral part of mission village work. The women taught vacation Bible schools after the regular schools had closed. They visited homes and also tended those who were ill — often bringing them on oxcarts to the hospital. If the preacher was away, a Bible woman led the service. She conducted village women's meetings and was often the only literate one in the group.

Many were the miles a Bible woman walked, sunshine or rain, often managing without food.

The following is the story of one such Bible woman, Gnanamma, formerly Laxmi.

At seven, Laxmi's parents married her to a reddi caste boy several years her senior. Before the final ceremony was performed, her husband-to-be died. Laxmi became a child-widow.

Singing attracted the child to the local Christian church. Despite her relatives' angry disapproval, Laxmi started attending services and was baptized at the age of twelve. Open confession infuriated her people and they threatened to abduct and kill her. Mr. and Mrs. E. Chute (missionaries in Mahbubnagar before we took over) moved Laxmi into their home. Her name was changed from Laxmi (goddess of wealth) to Gnanamma (wisdom) when she started attending the mission school. After she completed five or six forms and could read and write, she was sent to Nellore to enter the Women's Bible School. She completed three years there before graduating.

Gnanamma's wish was to return to Kauverampet, her village, to bring her people the Good News and teach them her Christian beliefs.

The missionaries helped her obtain a small plot of land near the village. Gnanamma's mother spat at her and called her "dog" which hurt Gnanamma but she never returned an angry word.

There was a very large boulder on Gnanamma's property which allowed no space for a hut. She didn't have enough money to have the rock removed or blasted. One chilly night, Gnanamma sat near the rock and built a small fire under a portion of the rock that protruded. She prayed fervently that God allow her some way to build a house on the small bit of property. For many hours she kept up a silent vigil next to her little fire. Figures glided past in the shadows murmuring and whispering at Gnanamma's strange behavior.

Tired after watching and praying, Gnanamma went to spend the rest of the night on a Christian neighbor's verandah.

During the night, it rained. At dawn, Gnanamma saw a crowd gathered around her property. To her astonishment, the rock had split in two. Villagers, who now thought Gnanamma possessed special powers, were eager to help her break up the rest of the rock. Soon a foundation was laid and some time later a small hut was built.

Gnanamma was still not allowed to draw water from the caste well. She had to wait for some other kindly soul to draw water for her.

One afternoon, she found no one at the well. Hot and thirsty, she let the rope down. Just then, a village man happened to be passing and shouted, "You are polluting our well." He smashed her pot into a thousand pieces and slashed her with the rope. Gnanamma responded to this abuse with "My Lord has suffered for me so I will not be offended."

That midnight, she heard coughing at her door. Fearfully asking the person's identity, Gnanamma found it to be the one who had abused her. He begged her to accompany him to his house to pray for his seemingly dying wife. Because she was a young widow, it was unwise and unsafe for her to leave her house. He may have wanted to seduce her or kill her, but after breathing a silent prayer, she followed the man to his hut.

There she found his wife indeed to be very, very ill. She had no medicine, but sponged the feverish woman, coaxing her to sip plenty of water. All the while she prayed.

With morning light, the woman responded and Gnanamma had the joy of leading two friends to her living God. Thus began the very useful service of a dedicated worker.

Stylized footsteps of the goddess Laxmi (wealth) used as designs in front of houses

En route to the Krishna River, and the place where Esther, John, Viola Ruth and Irene were baptized.

Father and Mother drove from Nagarkurnool to join us on the banks of the Krishna River. We had pitched our tents and had been camping for a few days. This Christmas season, 1939, was a special occasion. Our four oldest children were going to be baptized in the river on confession of faith in Christ. Grandpa, on the children's request, agreed to baptize them. Some Christians and Pastor M.S. Paul of the Amarchinta Village as well as interested Christians from Gadwal Field four miles away came early in the morning to be present.

Villagers who came to watch shook their heads from side to side in approval as our children, their Father and Grandfather entered the water. "Don't we all need to go into the holy waters to be purified?" "Wasn't the Krishna River one of the largest, named after the black Hindu diety and hero of the Indian epic Mahabharata?"

"Bathers in the River Krishna were lepers or high class Brahmins, Marvadis (merchants) or peasants, all devout Hindus. They submerged themselves to wash all sins away, after drinking the water and cupping their hands letting the water run through their fingers three times while saying their prayers."

While John, Father and the children entered the water, men, from a nearby village, swam around clapping their hands under water to frighten away crocodiles. The villagers had told us *tzaala jagrata undavallenu, pedda mossali unnavi* (Be very careful, there are big crocodiles). Women, they said, had been dragged into the water when they beat their clothes against the rocks or waded into the water to fill their *kundas* (pots). Hassan Ali Mirza, a Muslim friend of ours, shot a number of crocodiles for their hides. He found enough gold and silver ornaments in the stomachs of the animals to defray the expenses of his son's wedding!

After the baptism, the group of believers entered the larger of the two tents where Holy Communion was served and our children were accepted into the Family of God. Raisin juice, with a few drops of cochineal (made from dried insects) and sugar was poured into a glass and served from person to person. Pastor M.S. Paul broke *chapatis* (flat bread) and gave a piece to each participant. The short service was observed by many bystanders. We explained what baptism meant, that of following Christ's example of renewed life as Rom. 6:4 says: "We are buried with Him in baptism, that like Christ was raised from the dead, even so we, to walk in newness of life."

In any fairly large village, a number of self-contained communities each lived within its own well-defined area with its own forms of segregation. The dwellings were usually surrounded by a wall.

The wealthy and influential, such as the headman of the village, had at least five servants to do the work.

We hired a number of servants to do various tasks, partially because caste demarkation dictated this. This made a larger household unavoidable. The bearer who waited on the table and brought the food was not necessarily willing to cut the grass. Abraham, the cook, had his wife or another woman grind the spices for making curry and often the washing up. The sweeper dusted and swept the floors and also cleaned the latrines.

We had a cook, bearer, ayah (nurse), mali (gardener), Punkah walla (fan puller), and sweeper in that order. The cook received the highest salary, followed by the bearer and on down the scale.

Indian doras and dorasanis (master and mistress), often gave salaries "in kind." That meant a blanket a year, two meals a day and their clothing as well as a place to stay.

We inherited Abraham, a middle-aged jovial cook, from our parents when they went on furlough.

The family thought he was the best cook in the mission. When we complimented him on his dishes, his eyes shone as he said *vandanamulu* (thank you).

Because the kitchen was separate from the house, food had to be carried from there to the table. The iron woodburning stove had been new once, but parts of it were falling apart and had to be wired together. However, Abraham managed to make tasty food and now and then bake a cake in the tempermental oven.

Abraham was ever willing to accompany us on long tours in the villages. He improvised and cooked food over three stones, boiling drinking water which was then poured into earthen *kujas* (earthen pots) to cool. He found villagers willing to sell us buffalo milk (prefered to cow's milk because buffalo were less susceptible to tuberculosis) and eggs. The eggs were tested by putting them into a pan of cold water. If they floated, they were spoiled; if the eggs lay flat in the pan, they were good.

Abraham often made unleavened bread for us to eat with spicy curry. Rice or pudding was baked without an oven. Abraham put the pudding into a covered pan and placed hot coals on top of the lid and underneath the pan. The pudding slowly cooked. It was delicious.

Abraham was often seen talking to villagers as he squatted near the fire where he was cooking the food. He took time to tell them about the God he worshiped and the peace he had.

Some people dubbed him *chippalu nakevardu* (one who licks the plates). This did not please him. He was heard to say, "The food I cook is good. My *doragaru* and *ammagaru* trust me and eat my food, so what does it matter what you call me?"

Indeed, Abraham was a most trusted and devoted servant. We could not have continued our heavy schedules without his help. Often when it was mealtime, he would remind us, "You must come and eat."

Years later, Abraham became a preacher, sharing the "Bread of Life" with many.

Summers were often so hot that everything became combustible, dried out from heat and wind.

We visited one village in which ninety houses burned down. A spark from a cooking fire ignited the roof of one dwelling and the wind blew the fire through the village. Some tried to save their houses by pouring "water containing a gold object to prevent the house from catching fire" but to no avail.

Ankamma had been working in the field when her hut burned down. She was left with only the clothes she wore.

As we were talking to Ankamma she suddenly darted into a corner of what had been her home. She returned bringing two hands full of coins.

"These are the coins from the mitepot I had been saving for a year." Her tithe came to a considerable amount, about twenty rupees (at that time about $4.00). For a widow on *coolie* (day laborer) wages, this was a great deal.

We asked her why she didn't use any of this for herself. She said, "Oh no, what I have given to the Lord has been spared in the great fire. I will not use any of it. My God will take care of me."

Some time later, she took her offering to be counted with that of others at the Tettu Center.

"The heat has no caste favorites. Who will accuse a nation of poverty? And who will accuse a man of laziness? Who will feel pride in his charities or smugness in his work? — only he who is blind. Let such a man go to India in the hot season. Let him go with his high-minded zeal, with the knowledge that he understands the situation and can cure it. Let him hear the Lord as He speaks in the heat. And let him come home a humbler man." So writes David Toews in the "Herald" Vol. X, No. 16.

The morning sun hit us like a blow. The thermometer already had soared to 115 degrees. Although it was still early morning, people rested under the shade of Neem trees or near buildings, surrendering to the oppressive heat. Even the animals lay in whatever shade they could find, waiting for the afternoon when the scorching sun would relinquish control of the day.

Before making compound rounds to check on the work and visit any sick patients, John and I had pour baths and changed clothes yet again. We drank unsweetened lime juice on the verandah. Sweat ran down our bodies and the palms of our hands and elbows stuck to the wood frames of the chairs.

Evenings brought little relief. Those living on the compound often remarked on seeing John's office light burning late into the night and hearing his seemingly tireless fingers typing out mission reports, accounts and letters. During the still nights when sleep evaded us, we spread wet sheets on the stone floor of the bungalow and stretched out, sometimes taking a pour bath to stop the prickly heat itch.

The early morning, before dawn, was the best time of day during hot season. John and I ate our breakfast of fruit in season, toast and tea as the sun rose, promising another scorching day.

With government aid, Ankamma built a small hut after her house burnt down.

In *Foreign Missions, India,* published in April, 1948, I wrote:

"All too soon, school age comes and children must be separated from parents and their homes on the plains to go to boarding school.

"Our little missionaries have had superior advantages of travel in many countries among different people and races. They have learned to understand and appreciate people of many nationalities. They are advantaged because of their associations with other children of educated parents and who have grown up in consecrated homes.

"Thanks to those with a vision, schools on the hills in cooler climates have been established."

It was my turn to chaperone a group of Kodaikanal school children who were returning to their homes on the plains. After a day in Madras, we boarded a train and prepared ourselves for another overnight journey. During the night, I had violent diarrhea and vomiting and by morning I was quite weak with dehydration. Becoming worried, Esther, the oldest in the party of children, got off at one of the stations and ran alongside the train shouting, "Is there a doctor who can help?" A doctor specifically assigned to care for sick travelers and railway personnel came running to our compartment. He gave me an injection and stayed by my side until we reached Mahbubnagar station where John met us.

The children in our party came to spend the night with us. They all enjoyed a delicious dinner prepared with great care by cook Aaron. He was very deaf but accepted the children's shouted approval with a face glowing with gratitude.

Aaron had been a school boy in Kalvakurty but then was sent to study in Devarakonda. The teachers, not realizing that Aaron was deaf, thought him incapable of learning. His father, a preacher, asked John and me to find work for him. Aaron responded well to what I taught him in the kitchen and he became our cook.

Aaron proudly brought in the last course of the meal, a cream pie with meringue topping, the result of hours of careful preparation. The children, with obvious impatience, waited until the last person was served before taking a bite. Paul was the first to remark, "It tastes funny, Daddy." One by one, the children pushed back their plates without eating the pie. John took a bite of the pie and reacted by ordering all those who had eaten it to accompany him to the bathroom. There he put his finger down their throats and made them vomit what they had eaten.

Fortunately, there were no further bad effects but John accompanied the children who needed to travel further to Hyderabad. He took a sample of the tin of "cornstarch" to be analyzed by a chemist. Large amounts of carbolic acid were found and merchants were ordered to remove all tins of cornstarch from their shelves.

My twin son David's recollections:

"Leaving for school was always very sad. Although we knew it was inevitable, we tried to delay the departure by hiding. We were found but it made leaving a little less painful.

"Once at the station, all farewells said and our schoolmates started to join us at other stations, the sorrow of departure was forgotten.

"We had second class compartments with six or seven to a compartment. Pushing one another to enter, we *dubsed* (chose) our bunks for someone had to sleep on the floor which was none too clean. Bedrolls, in which we packed all linens, blankets, and towels needed at school, were unrolled. Then we prepared for the night and dozed off easily with the rocking motion of the train. Sometimes when the train stopped at stations, we visited other compartments, bought IJ (Indian junk) or fruit; bargained with and mimicked the *pawn* (bettlenut) and *beddie* (cigarette) vendors. The older boys stayed on the platform until the train moved and then daringly jumped on the windows or doors if they had been left open. (We closed the windows and doors because of the soot from the engine.)

Occasionally, we went to the engineer and asked for a ride in the engine. He let us ride to the next station and even pull the steam whistle.

"How hot the engine was! The stoker constantly shoved the coal into the great furnace and everything was covered with coal dust. Naked to the waist, stinking with sweat, they laughed at our attempts to put a few shovels of coal into the furnace.

"We had a through compartment to Dronachellum but had to change trains at Guntakal to larger carriages which were more comfortable. The Madras Mail took us to Madras Central Station.

"Arriving the next morning, we unloaded our *saaman* (luggage) and counted all the pieces. After a bit of haggling over prices, we hired coolies to carry the luggage to the waiting room.

"Taxis and rickshaws took us to Egmore Station where we met more schoolmates from other parts of India.

"The Trivandrum Express left in the evening so we had a day to enjoy in Madras. At 7:00 p.m., we again loaded our luggage and traveled to Kodai Road early in the morning. Then it was a rush to get the best seat in the first bus up the *ghat* (mountain road); preferably seats to the front of the bus as people vomiting out the canvas covered windows, was all too common."

Simple "Mugu"

Mugus are designs in front of village houses. After sweeping, the ground in front of the stoop is sprinkled with cowdung mixed with red dirt and water, and allowed to dry. Then the housewife sifts powdered lime through her fingers outlining the pattern of the *mugu*.

Lotus "Mugu"

"*Yemi cheystunnaru?* (What are you doing?)" I called to Subamma who was bent over as she deftly poured powdered lime through her fingers. In no time at all, she had made a beautiful design on the ground in front of her hut.

I sat down on the step of Subamma's hut while the Bible women accompanying me spoke with the others gathering around. Subamma's hair was still wet. She had just bathed in the nearby river before performing her morning *puja* (worship). Her mother-in-law sat nearby pounding the rice while her daughter ground the spices for curry.

"Are you going on any long journeys to visit your relatives?" I asked.

"I have to consult the *pujari* (priest) first to see when and what my horoscope says," Subamma said. (Many villagers are very superstitious and often don't have a major function or go on a long journey without first consulting an astrologer. The astrologer's work is to prepare a horoscope and make calculations for the future. He finds out the position of the planets and stars and then advises how this may affect plans such as a marriage date.)

"How much do you have to pay for his services?" was my next question.

"Sometimes we bring him rice or *ghee* (clarified butter) or a few rupees. He accepts anything we can give him, sometimes even a chicken or eggs."

Temples and holy places are often visited by villagers. Many of the nearby hills have temples with a pool where the pilgrims can bathe.

The villagers vary their religious practices. Some have personal gods and even take them along when they travel.

Is There A Spirit World?

"There is a spirit world," H.J. Harder wrote in *The Occult and the Bible*.

"Until recently, belief in an unseen spirit world was considered primitive, naive and superstitious . . ." Perhaps that is one reason that we who have seen demon possession feel reluctant to talk about it.

Two women came screaming and dancing towards us. We had just stopped the car at a *jatra* (fair). Our children were frightened and crouched low in their seats. John got out of the car and approached the women. In the name of the Lord Jesus Christ, he commanded the spirits to depart. The women became quiet and stood to listen while we talked to them about Christ who could free them from their bondage. Their "masters" came as in Acts 16 and were angry with us but the women *salaamed* (thanked) us and went away.

I was tired and hot so John and I sat down in the shade of a huge rock outcropping to rest. We had just climbed 300 steps to a temple on a hill where evangelists were distributing literature to those who could read. A woman who had been dipping herself in a stagnant pool below, came tottering towards an idol in the nitch of a boulder next to us. She started to shiver in the shade where the temperature was at least 108 degrees F. I went near her and tried to talk with her but she babbled something I could not understand. I put my hand on her dripping shoulder and said, "Amma, Jesus can help you. Would you like to know him?" At this, she stared at me and almost shouted, "I need help." She had a dry *sari* (women's cloth) lying near her, so I helped her dress and we sat and talked about her fears and troubles and about God's love in sending His Son to free her from the evil one.

Evil spirits opposing the evangelistic efforts were often felt. In one village, the singing and response had been particularly good during an evening meeting. Suddenly, a group of fellows started shouting and prancing about saying, "We don't want to hear of your God." The meeting was disrupted and the Christians left the village and literally shook the dust from their shoes.

This sign the villagers understood and some time later the village elders came and begged the Christian group to return and not leave a curse on their village. Those who had disturbed the meeting were ignorant, they said, and would not trouble us again.

Ephesians 6:12: "We wrestle not against flesh and blood but against principalities, powers, against rulers of this world and spiritual wickedness," but "Greater is He that is in you, than he that is in the world" 1 John 4:4.

We often heard, "She has the evil spirit," or "He is possessed." One Bible student, because she was often melancholy and depressed, was thought to be possessed. Her parents, an ignorant preacher couple, were also convinced of this. We found the parents pouring bucket after bucket of water on the girl's head from the rooftop. Drenched and wretched, the girl was sobbing quietly while tied to a post near the building. Her parents explained that a village doctor had told them to pour water on their daughter's head to rid her of the evil one.

We untied the wretched girl, dressed her in dry clothes and prayed with her. She later became the wife of a godly man who cared for her and helped her do outstanding work among village women.

Kodaikanal Lake on the Palni Hills, South India.

In the early 1940s, the Hieberts and we enrolled our children in Highclerc. This was a well established school in Kodaikanal, predominantly for missionary children. We had formerly had our oldest four children in the British system in Coonoor, where I went to school, but now John and I decided to introduce the children to the American curriculum.

Until early 1942, World War II had not affected us very much other than by the scarcity of basic commodities. Now, fighting in Europe was becoming much more intense. India feared an invasion because a Japanese fleet had been sighted off the coast of Madras.

John and I and other parents had been advised by the principal of Highclerc to take our children out of boarding. The possibility of roads, and therefore supplies, becoming cut off became too great a risk so we organized a "white exodus" as it was popularly called. Parents took their children down the *ghat* (mountain pass) in whatever transport they could find. My parents, who had come to Kodaikanal in May, took a bus. John and I, with our six children, together with the John Hieberts and their six children packed into our station wagon. A bag of shoes was tied to one fender and a bag of *topees* (pith helmets) to the other. We spread blankets in the back of the car to sit on and strapped canvas covered cases with clothes on the top of the car.

Winding down the *ghat*, the springs of the vehicle groaning, we stopped at fifteen-minute intervals to allow the cramped fussy children to stretch and run. While driving, John kept the children entertained with stories.

When we reached Mettur Dam Project on the plains, we uncoiled from our restricted positions and raced to the washrooms to pour cool water over ourselves. Temperatures were already exceeding 115° F and we were not accustomed to this heat. Mrs. Hiebert and I opened two tins of sardines and two of beans which were shared around with some bread for lunch before we proceeded further.

At dusk, we stopped near a *dak* (travelers) bungalow and opened more beans and sardines, the only tinned commodities available. John spread a large *tarpaulin* (canvas) on the ground and eight Hieberts stretched out on one end and eight Wiebes on the other until the gray light of dawn.

After four days of dust and heat, stopping often to repair blown tires or trying to find petrol which had become scarce even at black-market prices, we reached Mahbubnagar. The Hieberts continued on to Wanaparty.

Finally word came from Dr. C. Phelps, the principal of Kodaikanal School, that school would be reopened. I accompanied our children back to the hills in August, 1942. Mrs. P. Curtis and I rented Augustair Villa, a comfortable stone cottage a short distance from the school, where we lived together with the children. The Kodaikanal Municipality advised us to cover the doors and windows of our house at night when we lit a candle or lamp. Each of us had a little case with essential items packed and kept near our beds in the event of an emergency evacuation.

More and more soldiers wandered the streets of Kodaikanal as the war intensified. British and Indian troops took their leave of absence in the cool Palni Hills. Mothers were requested to move their children on or closer to the school premises. We occupied the school principal's vacant house near the lake and across the road from school. Soon it became necessary, as more and more teachers and school staff left Kodaikanal, for mothers to take on extra responsibilities. I became the housemother of thirty-eight girls ranging in ages from seven to eighteen. Esther, Ruth and Irene, resided in this dorm with me as well as our five-year old twins. John Jr. now and then climbed the fire escape and joined us for an evening.

Full blackouts were compulsory at night and we held frequent fire and emergency evacuation drills. The windows and doors of the dormitory were reinforced with bars. Air raid trenches were dug by the older children on the lower slope of the boys' dormitory to use in case of bomb attacks.

At the close of this tense school year, our children and I returned to John at Mahbubnagar for the Christmas holidays.

There was no radio communication in those days, but letters were received from the American Consulate saying that all Americans should leave India. The American Government said they could no longer be responsible for our safety.

The Lohrenzes, my parents, and we decided to stay in India. Our Indian friends and colleagues told us that they needed us and would hide us if necessary. The Hieberts, Unruhs, and Dicks from the Mennonite Mission heeded the Consular's advice and left as soon as passage was available on the *S.S. Gripsholm*. A measles outbreak, blackouts and mines planted in the sea made this a very difficult voyage. When asked by the Mennonite Brethren Mission Board why the Wiebes didn't return with the others to America, someone reported that "they were afraid to travel during the war!"

Kodaikanal Bazaar

ILLUSTRATED BY BRUCE PECK

We hosted the annual Mennonite Brethren Mission Conference in Mahbubnagar in 1943.

I dreaded conferences. There were so many arrangements to be made in order to house and feed thirty-five to forty people for four days. It was a strain on our tight budget to be the host family but we managed by serving vegetables and fruit from our garden. The missionaries brought their own cots and bedding. School was closed for the holidays so we housed our guests in empty classrooms.

I considered having squab for dinner the first night of the conference but found that Esther had locked the door of the pigeon house so no one could enter. After we managed to pry open the door, we found the kitchen knives missing. To satisfy our determined daughter, I had some chickens butchered for the meal which still caused anguish. Our children had names for all their pet chickens, monkey, cows, buffalo, cats and dogs and cared for them faithfully.

By and large, the mission conference group was congenial. At many meetings, future mission strategies such as the need to relinquish leadership to nationals as soon as possible and the necessity of adapting to changing conditions were discussed — sometimes with harsh words and disagreements.

Missionaries were not immune to problems. Small weaknesses which may not have been apparent in the homeland were often compounded on the field. The restrictions and pressures of the field created situations that brought out the worst in people's dispositions. There was little or no privacy. Missionaries were often strong willed, aggressive people, characteristics which carried them through difficult times with a determination to succeed in spite of obstacles and hardships.

Living conditions of missionaries were comparatively high to the vast majority of people around them, but nevertheless, inferior to what most missionaries had been accustomed to in their homeland with regards to availability of certain types of food and equipment. Because there were often water problems, many missionaries suffered from the summer's oppressive heat which was very enervating.

At one meeting, I raised the suggestion that it was time to start a Women's Association. To have women from all nine Mennonite Brethren Mission fields meet together to chal-

lenge each other and have spiritual discussions away from mundane chores and household tasks. Many of the Indian women were eloquent speakers and teachers but had little opportunity to express themselves. The money collected from the women would then be spent for projects for widows and orphans.

Some of the single missionary women agreed with the idea. Other missionaries opposed it saying that such a conference would encourage the women to neglect their family responsibilities and would interfere with wives' attitudes towards their husbands. After much discussion, we decided to try out the meetings, which proved to be very successful.

A program in which the children performed, was planned for the last evening of the conference. Eight little Unruhs, Wiebes, Hieberts and Dicks paraded into the room where the adults were seated, bringing with them a large dry branch to which cherry-sized red tomatoes were tied. They danced around the tree singing a song Viola Ruth composed: "Cherry blossom apple tree, see how it bears for you and me."

Hearty group singing followed. Strength and inspiration came from studying some passages from the Word and praying together, sharing a common purpose despite individual differences. Farewells were then said in anticipation of early morning departures for various stations.

My birthday was approaching and another "gift" was due. John joined me in Kodaikanal prior to the birth of our seventh child. As I was past forty years of age, Dr. Anna Otto, the Van Allen Hospital Superintendent, advised me to enter the hospital a little earlier than the date of the expected delivery. I was checked into the "blue room" overlooking the dramatic view of the plains 7000 feet below. Dr. Otto attended me at the birth of our daughter, Marilyn Susanne, on 18 August 1943.

When the birth of a sister was announced to the twins they rushed home from school and chorused, "Not another dame!" Nevertheless, there were plenty of sibling hands ready to care for the little girl. We now celebrated five Wiebe birthdays in the month of August.

After ten days, I was strong enough to be discharged from the hospital and we moved into a cottage at Furzbank, the property of the Methodist mission. The house was vacant as most of the missionaries had gone to their work on the plains. It was a cozy rock cottage. When the children came home from school, we ate our suppers around a blazing fire because the air was cool and crisp. After several days of rest and quiet, John left us and returned to Mahbubnagar.

It was difficult to be separated from John for long periods of time. His workload also became heavier as he took over my responsibilities as well as his own. One of these was caring for the sick school boarders. John was pleased to write to me of the improved condition of the boarders after Devasahayam had used an ayurvedic cure of minerals and herbs to cure the boys' sores. Devasahayam (God's helper) was a Christian from Manganur and knew a great deal about ayurvedic medicine.

Now that many big school and community functions were finished for the season, there was time to read Kipling or Alcott to the children after homework and before devotions. After housekeeping chores were finished there was time to write letters to long neglected friends and articles for periodicals. Authors such as Shakespeare, Scott, Marshall, Sheldon and Hawthorne, which had long graced our bookshelves, but were seldom opened were now avidly read. Music, too, was a part of our enjoyment. The children made "comb" music, played harmonicas and made a joyful sound on Father's accordion.

In October, we traveled down together to John in Mahbubnagar for the Christmas holidays.

The Harvest Field is printed once in three months at the American Mennonite Brethren Mission Press, Mahbubnagar, Deccan, India. Annual subscription: eight annas.

HARVEST FIELD

Editor: John A. Wiebe.

MORE LABOURERS ARE NEEDED!!

1945 MISSION FIELD STATISTICS

THE FIELD
Square Miles	10000
Population	1500000
Villages	1800
Villages with Christians	600

EVANGELIZATION
Ordained preachers	11
Licensed preachers	132
Village teachers	115
Bible women	100
Bible students	30

CHURCHES
Baptized in 1945	550
Baptized believers	12500
Organized churches	57
Buildings for church services	57
Contributions	$2130 Rs. HS 8110

COMPOUND SCHOOLS
High School boys	60
High School girls	21
Middle School boys	162
Middle School girls	138
Elementary School boys	333
Elementary School girls	297
Teachers	51

VILLAGE SCHOOLS
Number of Schools	150
Children studying	1900
Adults studying	450

MEDICAL WORK
Trained workers	15
Number of inpatients	2364
Number of outpatients	27692
Beds in hospitals	60

MISSIONARIES
Men missionaries 1945	5
Women missionaries 1945	11

The figures give the summary of the statistics supplied by the missionaries of the different stations. We thank the Lord for blessings given in the work.

Printed at the A. M. B. Mission Press, Mahbubnagar, Deccan, India.

While in middle school in Nagarkurnool, B. Aseervadam showed unusual talent and interest in the printing work Father started. Father trained him and gave him responsible jobs such as setting type by hand and running the linotype machine. When my parents left for America, the press was transferred to Mahbubnagar. John became the manager and B. Aseervadam the foreman. The press struggled with lack of proper funding and collecting the yearly subscription rate of eight annas.

The *Suvarthamani* (Telugu monthly paper) and the *Harvest Field* (English Quarterly), books, pamphlets and many jobs for mission, church and school were printed on the press.

John, like his father-in-law, was convinced that literacy was necessary. A quote from a letter John wrote to the mission board states: "I believe it will interest thinking friends of the mission to know what the actual literacy situation is in the Nizam's Dominion of India in the 1940s.

"Only fifty out of every thousand inhabitants in the State can read. The figures for the Christian population show much better progress. About 20 percent or two hundred out of every thousand Christians in the State can read and write.

"We have good reason to believe that soon a much larger percentage of Christians, at least, shall be literate. The prejudice towards women's education is slowly being overcome. Children in remote villages are also learning to read. Literacy is on the increase and good Christian literature should keep pace with the increasing demand."

A new memorial building erected with funds from friends and family in America was dedicated to Rev. Daniel Bergthold, my Father, when the rooms for the heavy machinery, cutting and binding, and small reading room were completed.

Pastor M.B. John and workers Y. Daniel, M. Zachariah and foreman, B. Aseervadam, school children and staff gathered for the dedication. A large picture of the founder, Father, was hung. The press was now ready to expand to serve a wider clientele.

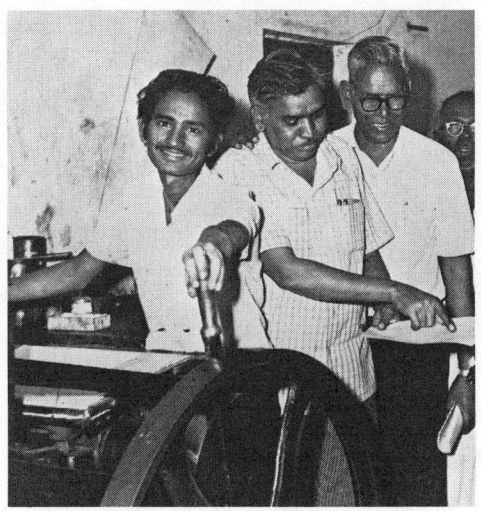

In press building, M. Zachariah, helper, B. Aseervadam, foreman, Rev. M.B. John, pastor

At the dedication of the Bergthold Memorial Press building

I wrote in a Foreign Mission Journal:

"Children see the years of toil and sacrifices that their fathers and mothers have known. The challenge of every nerve and talent, the pouring out of the soul. Is it any wonder that they, too, have a part in being little missionaries?"

In a letter to the Wiebe parents in Minnesota, John wrote:

"Viola and our daughters, Esther, Viola Ruth, Irene, Marilyn. To me it is a good picture. Thanks be to God for children. And for my beloved life's companion.

With love from your son and daughter and grandchildren,"

John

India

My parents retired from active mission work in India in 1946. John accompanied them to Calcutta where they were to board a ship. I remained with the twins and Marilyn in Mahbubnagar.

These are excerpts from a letter dated 29-1-46 written by my Father to us:

"Astoria Hostel
"Calcutta

"Dear child Viola and grandchildren!

Thank you very dear Viola for your glad consent to be quite alone while John accompanied us on the long journey. Without John to bear such burdens as come with a long railway journey at this time, especially when a speedy change was necessary at Wardha and Nagpur, the transference of luggage, the finding of a place to lodge in a city which seems to be overfilled, we would have had quite a different story to tell you after but a very few days of separation.

". . . If John had not been called to preach the Gospel when he was, he would have become one of the most renowned diplomats in this wicked world.

". . . John has become a missionary and will, I feel, certainly remain such and his many talents will not be wasted in that glorious vocation. In the presence of his vigorous and alert mind and strong physical power, I feel that I have become older than I was willing to own and it becomes proof to me that we have made no mistake in entrusting the burdens that we tried to bear into another's hands.

". . . We are glad, although we must now and for all time turn, as it were, our backs on India, we have such precious children, to remain and continue in the land which has become to us much more than the land of second choice.

"In tenderest bonds of love we are and ever will be,"

Mother & Father

The following was written by John in an article titled "Journeying Mercies," relating our travels in 1946:

"We were advised to go on furlough so applied for passage in June of 1946. In a war-torn world, getting passage for a family of nine was not an easy matter. We thank authorities for arranging for our home-going on the steamship *General Gordon* in the month of August.

"Our faithful friends and fellow workers and with them the many boys and girls prayed for us upon leaving. Amidst a farewell and *salaams* (greetings), we left our station and home in India.

"The harbor city of Bombay seemingly had no place for us to lodge. Finally, we found room in a day school. We cooked on a hot plate and it was the first and likely the last time in life that all members of the family slept on tables with what little bedding we had.

"After six days of a tiresome sojourn in the city, the ship, flying the stars and stripes, docked and we boarded with 1500 others.

"It hurt to leave India."

We would have liked to travel on the ship in one class as a family, but considered it fortunate to have accommodation at all. The four girls and I were given a cabin in officer's class together with thirteen other women.

John, with our three sons, slept with a hundred men in the troop holds where bunks were five deep. The heat was sometimes unbearable in the lower cabins and John and the boys stayed on the ship's deck as much as possible.

We sailed straight into a heavy storm and the steamer lurched and rolled. Passengers vomited in the halls and even in the drinking fountains. One poor person, finding all the toilets full, found the officer's toilet vacant and vomited there. A steward, exasperated by now with cleaning up, grabbed the miserable vomiting man, pushed his head into the toilet bowl, and flushed the pot.

Strained and impatient, we stood in a long queue waiting for breakfast one morning. Suddenly, a well dressed European woman slapped her bowl of porridge into the face of a short, dark Indian man. He fell and she pounded him with her shoe until they were separated. A few days later, a Chinese, who had lost heavily while gambling, was found hanging in a room next to the large state room.

After a few more days of raging seas, calm weather made the voyage much more comfortable. Passengers could stroll on the decks and the atmosphere became much more relaxed. That is until we saw the masts, funnels and the wreckage of ships in Manila Harbor. The city also was in ruins. Buildings were broken and jumbled together with rusted metal forming abstract images against the sky. Our family together with nine others jammed into a reconditioned jeep and toured the city. When we returned to the ship, we found many little makeshift boats huddling the steel sides of the *S.S. General Gordon*. Hungry men held up their hands towards the ship anticipating discarded food.

A few days later, we climbed the hills on the Island of Hong Kong. Many homes had been looted and were deserted. The ravages of war were evident everywhere.

After twenty-eight days, the *General Gordon* sailed under the Golden Gate Bridge of San Francisco. Some of John's relatives, Jake, a brother, and his wife, Lydia; Emma, his sister, and her husband, Peter Friesen, came to the pier to meet us.

There was a dock strike, so no porters were there to help carry passengers' luggage. Our family struggled slowly down the gangplank with what we could carry. One of the porters, seeing brother Jake approaching, said, "Hey, we ain't working." To which Jake, a hardworking Minnesota farmer, retorted, "I ain't done a lick of work all my life, why would I start now?" With that, he helped carry the heavier luggage down the gangplank.

After customs, John's family took us to Reedley, California, where others awaited our arrival.

MISSIONARY CREDENTIAL

To Whom this May Concern:

REV. P. R. LANGE
CHAIRMAN
HILLSBORO, KANSAS

REV. G. B. HUEBERT
FIRST VICE CHAIRMAN
REEDLEY, CALIFORNIA

REV. H. S. VOTH
SECOND VICE CHAIRMAN
WINKLER, MANITOBA

REV. JOHN A. HARDER
RECORDING SECRETARY
YARROW, B. C.

REV. A. E. JANZEN
EXECUTIVE SECRETARY
AND TREASURER
HILLSBORO, KANSAS

REV. G. D. PRIES
ASSISTANT TREASURER
WINKLER, MANITOBA

MISSION FIELDS

AFRICA
BELGIAN CONGO

CHINA

INDIA

NORTH AMERICA
AMONG
INDIANS
MEXICANS
RUSSIANS

SOUTH AMERI
BRAZIL
COLOMBI
PARAGU

This is to certify that Rev. and Mrs. John A. Wiebe are ordained missionaries of the Mennonite Brethren Church of North America and are serving in India under the direct appointment and support of the BOARD OF FOREIGN MISSIONS. This Board assumes all responsibility for the expenses of Rev. and Mrs. Wiebe and their children, their traveling expenses, salaries, and other costs arising in connection with their work and duties on the mission field, as well as their eventual repatriation.

The Board wishes to state further that all baggage which the Wiebes are taking with them is strictly for personal use and that no articles are being taken along for resale in the United States or any country enroute.

Respectfully,

A. E. Janzen
Executive Secretary
Board of Foreign Missions

Given at Hillsboro, Kansas
April 2, 1946

A city street scene

A friend from U.S.A. with our family and Mother in Nagarkurnool

The pastor of the large Reedley Mennonite Brethren Church, Rev. G.B. Huebert, invited our family to present the work of missions in India the first Sunday after we had arrived in America. Before the service closed, the pastor encouraged all nine of us to stand up on the stage. He then explained to the congregation that we had been representing them in India for the past ten years. He informed the congregation that the collection that day would be used to purchase each of us a pair of shoes. For this we were very grateful.

We enjoyed the warmth of California but an urgent call came from Kansas insisting that we attend a mission Harvest Festival. We boarded a train as soon as we could for the midwestern plains and the beginning of cold, frosty weather.

Our family participated in the mission festival service with speeches, songs and slides of the work in India. While John was showing the pictures, the pastor abruptly left the meeting and went home, leaving us to end the service with a closing prayer. Later when we returned to the house, the pastor confronted us with "You showed a picture of your girls wearing pants. I have been trying for months to influence the women of the church not to wear men's clothing and you have spoiled my teaching."

We packed our suitcases for an early morning departure to Hillsboro, a small college town in Kansas. There we joined our parents, the Bergtholds, in a joyful reunion. After a few days, we continued on to our final destination, Mountain Lake, Minnesota.

It was the first time a home church had arranged for a rent-free house for missionaries to live in. We were grateful to move into the two-story clapboard house, a haven after our travels. We kept the potbelly stove stoked and pushed paper into the cracks of the doors and windows to keep out the chill winter air. There was a cistern under the house from which our water supply was pumped. We drank the water until we found tadpoles swimming in our glasses. Soon after this, pipes from the city main supply were installed in the house and we were advised to use the cistern water only for washing.

John escorted the six oldest children to school the first day of classes and introduced them to their teachers and principal one by one. It had been ten years since we had been in America and the children found their clothes made by the village *dergi* (tailor) in India quite different from their new friends. Our three girls were mortified when they were told that their homemade underwear looked like it came from "Noah's Ark."

In a letter to my parents in India, John wrote:

"On the tenth of October, we came to our journey's end, Mountain Lake, Minnesota. We stepped from the train at the very spot where ten years ago we boarded the same train. Father and Mother, brothers and sisters, friends and relatives met us with a song.

"Seated around the table at the parental home, we talked of the blessing God gives. Of journeying mercies. Our seven children have been brave. They were always ready to meet trials. We thank the Lord for their many smiles in times of inconveniences."

The children and I lived in Mountain Lake while John studied in the Lutheran Northwestern Seminary. He traveled home on weekends when he was not preaching in churches. John earned the reputation of being a "Francis of Assisi" with his gentle spirit and caring for those in need. He taught German to students in the seminary to supplement our family's income. In the Spring of 1948, John received his Bachelor of Divinity.

The following year, he rented a room in a dwelling house while attending the University of Minnesota in Minneapolis. There he studied for and received his Masters in Anthropology.

Artist: Louis E. Ulrich.

BACHELOR OF DIVINITY

Robert B. Anderson

Merle G. Franke

John H. Gerberding

Carl E. Oslund

James D. Reid

Howard A. Rice

Louis E. Ulrich

John A. Wiebe

Victor K. Wrigley

Lloyd W. Zaudtke

Northwestern Lutheran Theological Seminary

Minneapolis, Minnesota

Class of 1948

Packing our Chevrolet station wagon with a few suitcases and bedding, the nine of us began the often tiring trip of traveling from church to church. The mission board had told us that after our family presentations in the Mennonite Brethren Churches, contributions for the work in India increased substantially.

Distances between churches were long and we often spent the night in the open beside the car. Spreading a tarpaulin on the ground, each of us rolled up in his or her blanket on the canvas with the stars as our canopy.

Traveling on, we stopped at whatever filling station or National Park facility was available to wash up. With very little money to spend on food, we bought a loaf of bread, cold meat and cheese and a large tin of tomato or orange juice. Esther, the oldest, and I sat in the middle seat of the station wagon and prepared sandwiches, passing them to the driver and to those sitting in the back. The tin of juice was then passed around for each person to take a gulp. Sometimes we purchased a crate of fresh tomatoes or fruit to eat along the way.

Eating like this became monotonous so now and then we stopped at a small town restaurant to order a hot meal. Being as poor as the proverbial "church mice," we couldn't choose the best places to eat. John, particular about the quality of food we ate, inspected the restaurant's kitchen to see how and what was cooking. At times, he marched all nine of us out of the restaurant saying, "We can't eat here!" Young John sometimes balked at walking into public places with the rest of us, preferring to eat bread and fruit in the car.

Because there were nine of us, we were separated into three or four homes for meals and the night when we reached the town or church where we were to speak. Usually the three boys were assigned to one home, the three girls to another and Marilyn with John and me.

Generally, the evening service was ours to do with as we pleased. Looking around from one white face to another white face in a meeting, little Marilyn, who was only three, said, "There are only uncles and aunties here, where are all the people?"

After John had given a meditation, I, wearing a sari (the dress of Indian women), talked about children and women's work. Many members of the congregation had been interested in mission work for half a century and we wanted them to be assured that their "giving" and prayers were not in vain.

The children, dressed in costumes from various parts of India, gave short descriptions of the people he or she represented and an incident or story about them. Many times people told us that our children's participation in the services helped encourage their young people. Interspersed, we sang our family theme songs: "When I Survey the Wondrous Cross," "This is My Father's World," and our Telugu favorite — *Devuni Preyma Idigo* ("Behold the Love of God"). John then showed slides of the many aspects of the work on the field. As soon as the lights were switched off, the twins stretched out on the front benches and went to sleep.

During one of the meetings, a distraught Irene said, "Daddy, the same people that were here two nights ago are here again. What shall I talk about tonight?" John suggested she tell about the white ants. When it was Irene's turn to speak, she stood up and told how destructive white ants were and that "they ate holes in my clothes I left on the floor over night!" She hurriedly ended her little speech with "Please pray for them," which brought a few jabs in the ribs and stifled laughter from the rest of us.

Tiring of the long after-meeting greetings and talking, our youngest went to the car and sang her repertoire of songs. An old man, amused, offered her a quarter. From then on, after every meeting, little Marilyn ran out to the car to sing after meetings hoping for a handout.

A friend, Rev. John Janzen, found work for our family in Salem, Oregon, with a fruit

grower who was willing to hire us along with other itinerant pickers for the summer of 1949. We packed our bags and headed for the West Coast.

After reaching Salem, we rented a shabby two-room house with porches, about a half hour's car ride from the city. Here the nine of us managed to sleep on bunk beds and cots which kind people from the church lent us. There was a little stove that came with the house on which we prepared early morning breakfasts and lunches to take along to the fields where we picked fruit in season.

The first few weeks we came home bedraggled and tired after eight or nine hours of crawling on our knees picking strawberries. Next came cherries. Lovely Bings and sour ones. To encourage ourselves, we sang as we ate (for we were allowed to eat as many as we wanted), "Get up the tree and eat them all, cherries bright and cherries small, cherries, cherries." Beans were next. Rows and rows of them and then, for a short while, loganberries.

At summer's end, the orchard owners allowed us to pick the culls from the various orchards which John and son John canned. We bought a small trailer to pack our tins of beans, strawberries and cherries and returned to the midwest with enough cash to last us through another winter.

The children enjoyed visiting the family farm with their grandparents. Father Wiebe, always cheerful, told them stories of what their Daddy did when he was a young boy on the farm. Father did much visitation even though he had retired from his ministerial position which he had held for forty years in the Carson Mennonite Brethren Church.

Mother Susie Wiebe died while we were in India. Father married Helen Dick several years later and then the two of them spent three years together in Mountain Lake, Minnesota.

Mother called us one evening saying, "Come quickly, I need you." John and I hurried over to their little house and found Father Wiebe lying across the threshold of the dining room where he had fallen after gathering eggs in the hen house.

Father was seventy-four when he breathed his last, for when John and I lifted him onto the sofa, we found his soul had gone home to the Lord whom he had served faithfully. With all his children and many friends in attendance he was buried in the Carson cemetery. We were glad that we could be with Mother during those difficult days.

During the summer of 1948, we had a joyful visit with my parents in Alhambra, California. They had retired and now lived near their sons Henry and Sam and daughter Martha, and their families.

We had not been back in Minnesota long when John flew to Reedley, California to attend General Conference Meetings. While there, he had a telephone call from Mother Bergthold in Alhambra, asking him to come quickly as Father was not well.

While sitting outside in their lovely garden the next morning, Father quietly handed John his notebook in which he kept his sermon notes with the words, "I was to speak in the Los Angeles church on Sunday, but I won't need this book anymore." With the words still on his lips, he lay his head back and went to Glory.

I flew to Los Angeles for the funeral attended by all of Father's children. The internment took place in Rosehill Cemetery, Los Angeles. Representatives from the Mission Board and several churches were present to bury one who had given his all to the Lord's work in India.

Left: Father and Mother Wiebe in Minnesota
Right: Our family with Father and Mother Bergthold in Alhambra, CA., in their garden, weeks before Papa died.

Packing our accumulated belongings after living in Minnesota for two years, we prepared to leave for Kansas. There, John would be teaching in Tabor College, Hillsboro, and the four oldest would be attending classes in Tabor College.

On a warm summer day, just before leaving, our twin sons David and Paul were baptized by Rev. Dan Friesen and Rev. Bill Neufeld in a small lake, near Mountain Lake.

In Hillsboro, we rented a four-bedroom drafty house that had stood vacant for a long time. It was opposite the town park and near the college. The previous occupant had thrown her tin cans and bottles down the stairs into the basement. It took some time to clean the house before we felt like living in it.

Esther graduated from college in 1951 and continued as secretary to Rev. A.E. Janzen, the General Secretary of the Mennonite Brethren Mission. The same year, John Jr., was in his last year of college, Viola Ruth was a sophomore and Irene a freshman in Tabor.

During our family devotions one morning, John and I asked our four oldest children, "Are you willing we leave you and return to the mission field in India." To our concerned question, for it wasn't easy to leave the children behind, they replied, "The people in India need you."

It was a rainy year in Kansas; rivers were in spate and basements flooded because of the high water level. Our trunks were packed and ready to go and stored in the basement. One morning, to our dismay, we saw the trunks floating in water. There was nothing to do but salvage what we could; to wash and dry the clothing and bedding when the sun came out. The four children staying in America needed their share of linens and blankets. The three accompanying us to India were traveling directly to boarding and needed their things packed separately. John's and my belongings would be going to Mahbubnagar.

Finally we were repacked and ready to begin our journey back to India after living in America for five years.

Our last formal family picture before leaving for India on the *S.S. Billiton*.

Dr. Roy Just lent our four oldest children a car and gave them $50 so they could accompany us to New Orleans where we were to board the *S.S. Billiton* for India. Captain Van de Meer allowed five of us to sleep in our cabin berths on the ship, the other four members of our family slept in a motel for two nights before we sailed.

We enjoyed touring the fine old city of New Orleans before the evening of our departure. Then, driving to the outskirts of the city, we bid farewell to our four oldest after prayers and many tears and watched them join the speeding traffic back to Kansas, committing them to our Lord's protection.

We boarded a bus and took our three youngest back to the port. Here we boarded the cargo ship which carried twelve passengers. Missionaries Dr. J. Friesens, Rev. J. Kasper and Jack, his son, had boarded earlier. (Rev. Kasper's wife, Eva, had drowned with her small son while crossing the Krishna River in India the year before.)

On that relaxing two-month trip, John taught the Friesens Telugu and I taught Jack and our three youngsters from schoolbooks we had brought along.

While sailing through the Persian Gulf, Dr. J. Friesen received a cablegram that his Father who had accompanied them to New Orleans, had died. Captain Van de Meer arranged for a memorial service to be held in the lounge which those who were seaworthy attended.

Excerpts from John Wiebe's diary, 1951, '52:
"The Coasts of Tyre and Sidon and Christmas and New York in the Persian Gulf"

Nine representatives of the Mennonite Brethren Mission together with fifty three other persons including crew were passengers on the steamer. On 28 November 1952, the Dutch *S.S. Billiton* quietly slipped down the Mississippi Delta. The small group of missionaries together with as many who wanted to attend, met in the lounge for meditation and worship. The steamer sailed straight east toward the coasts of Tyre and Sidon.

Long before the ship cast anchor, we could see the Lebanon Mountains outlined against the eastern horizon. While looking at the green slopes, our thoughts were of Christ who visited these coasts many years ago.

The *S.S. Billiton*, which registered seventeen knots an hour on high sea, slowed down as it neared the breakwater of Beirut Harbor. It was just before sundown. Soon thousands of lights along the shores and slopes of the mountains lit up the growing port city which has been referred to as the "Gateway of Asia."

Since 1918, Beirut has been the capital of Lebanon and has become a great metropolis. The inhabitants speak Arabic. Because of the French mandate over a period of years, many speak French. We again realized how limited our medium of communication is when we speak only one or two languages.

The *S.S. Billiton* docked for a week. We were privileged to drive up the western slope of the Lebanon Mountains on the Rue Damascus. While descending into the fertile plains, we saw Mt. Hermon and then drove north to the world famous ruins of Baalbeck. One wonders how the Phoenicians quarried and moved stone blocks weighing from 750 to 1200 tons. There are three limestone blocks, each measuring approximately sixty-four feet in length, fourteen feet in height and twelve feet in breadth. It has been calculated that the combined efforts of 40,000 men would be required to move these enormous stones.

After viewing the ruins, we drove to a park through which flow streams of water from springs on the slopes of the Anti-Lebanon Range. We spread our blankets on green grass and had lunch. Soon Arab vendors came to sell us their unique souvenirs.

Before sunset, we again reached the highest point leading over the Lebanon Mountains. Our guide pointed out the new large airport on the shores of the Mediterranean, in contrast to the ruins of Baalbeck.

The next day, the missionary Willoughbys invited us to accompany them to Keyam in the southeast corner of Lebanon. The winding mountain road led us by the Beaufor Castle which was built on a commanding precipice by the crusaders about 800 A.D. The Arabs at the meeting told us about battles which raged in the Hullie lowlands in the recent war with Israel. 800,000 Arabs were driven from their homes and not permitted to return owing to continued tension between the two countries. After the council meetings, we experienced genuine Lebanese hospitality. Over stony paths, where generations have stumbled, we watched our step until we were heartily welcomed into a house adjoining the rugged road. While enjoying the savory rice with olives, mutton and vegetables, we broke unleavened bread not far from where Christ fed the 5000. Sweet oranges and bananas were passed around again and again. We were glad for the fine "love feast" the Ghanam family shared with us.

The third of December, we brought a fourteen inch long warm loaf of bread, ham, cheese and oranges and picnicked at the American University campus. Thousands of eager students from surrounding countries as well as from Lebanon attended the University.

The moon and stars were beautiful on the night of 5 December when we arrived at Port Said. Our ship anchored alongside other ships. All were waiting for the convoy to start through the Suez Canal. On the following morning, our ship quietly sailed through the desert.

British troops stationed at important centers along the canal were the only indication of tension in Egypt. After a beautiful sunset, we sailed past the disturbed city of Ismalia and into the Gulf of Suez.

On 9 December, we were invited to the bridge to get a good view of the large masses of protruding rocks which are commonly referred to as the twelve apostles. On the 10th, we anchored at the Port of Aden to refuel.

This gave us time to go ashore. We took a taxi and drove a distance of ten miles on roads which were blasted through along steep sides of Aden's hills of solid rock. On previous trips, we have found this area unbearably hot but during this winter voyage, ocean breezes have been cool.

Fourteen December, we sailed through the Strait of Ormuz and into the Persian Gulf. I spent some time on the bridge from where both coasts were visible: Persia to the right and Oman to the left. Many workers scrambled on deck climbing up ropes with both fingers and toes, helping to unload American power wagons. The rapidly growing oil industry requires more and more vehicles.

The next day was cloudy and somewhat foggy. Later it rained while the captain directed the heavily laden ship towards the head of this great gulf. Buoys indicated that dangerous reefs were to the right and left of our course. On the Lord's Day, blinking buoys reminded us that "Ye are the light of the world." We anchored at Ras Tanura. Great fires burning waste gasses indicated the place where postwar refineries were located. The world's largest oil pipeline, measuring thirty one inches in diameter, connected the wells with Sidon of Lebanon.

Monday evening, the gulf took its toll. The sea was rough. A tug pulling the lighters, one behind the other, was making its way around the bend of the coast only about a quarter of a mile from where our ship lay anchored. A smaller motorboat, evidently attached to the last barge, suddenly capsized and its crew of six was thrown into the foaming sea. Five were rescued but the driver sank with the boat.

During the night of the 18th, the *S.S. Billiton* sailed to the docks of Bahrein Island. Two warships anchored near our moorings, reminded us of present-day tension in the gulf. Puffing tugs helped us start on Sunday morning, 23 December and soon the *Billiton* sailed into a foggy sea. It was surprisingly cool at the head of the gulf and no wonder for we were sailing about 30 degrees north latitude. We anchored about four miles from Kuwait the day before Christmas. On Christmas morning, we were still anchored at Kuwait.

All on board were invited to attend the season's programme. Dutch carols were heartily sung, the children performed and I preached to an attentive audience on "Good Tidings of Great Joy." Following the service, Captain Van de Meer distributed presents to all members of the ship's personnel.

The missionary DeJongs invited us to visit Kuwait. Owing to wind and high waves, we found it difficult to board the little craft that was heaving near the gang way. Viola stepped off the ladder just as the boat sank with the wave. The Arab man who had taken her hand grabbed her and they swayed over the side of the boat, precariously close to feeding the sharks. A sigh of relief was heard from each as we found shelter behind the breakwater in the little harbor for small boats after our five-mile trip to the shore.

We crawled up the crude embankment to find cars winding their way around donkeys, horses and mules. The well-to-do class affected a dignified appearance as they paraded along crowded streets in their black and white turbans and togas. Corrugated iron roofs built over narrow streets for blocks on end were for the purpose of protecting shoppers from the heat of the sun. We were surprised to learn that all of Kuwait's drinking water was shipped in from other ports.

Still remembering our trying experience we had coming from the *Billiton*, we hesitantly boarded the flattopped craft with a good measure of concern. For another twenty-five minutes, we were again tossed about on turbulent waters. We were thankful to return to the *Billiton* and an elegant Christmas dinner.

On 26 December, the ship cut across the head of the Persian Gulf and nosed its way up the River Khor Musa to the docks at Bandar Shapur, made famous during the last World War. It was here that American boys were disembarked and entrusted with the responsibility of building docks and tracks to make possible quick delivery of war and food supplies to Russia.

The snowcapped mountains to the east clearly visible on bright mornings afforded us an inspirational view. They proclaimed the power and majesty of our Creator.

Countless date palms, to the right and to the left, indicated that we were now sailing up the great Shatt el Arab River. Our ears were all attention when officers informed us that the smokestacks of the world famous

Abadan refinery were in sight. From the bridge, we had a good view of this great industrial center. Today Abadan is very quiet. Docks, where dozens of tankers once received oil simultaneously, now are places for idle workers to congregate and watch the great ships pass. How a place of unlimited productivity can become a place of inactivity in such a short time is difficult to comprehend. Tension and strife between nations leads to inevitable loss.

We watched the Margil docks at Bahsrah the last day of the year. Soon large cranes were groaning while heavy cargo was being transferred from the five hatches of the ship to the docks. On the first of the year, we were privileged to visit the Iraqian home of the Essayes, the manager of the Garibian Company at Bahsrah. They showed their kind hospitality by sharing with us chocolate and manna. Mr. Essaye took us through a vacant palatial home standing near by. Again, we saw the great contrast between the rich and the poor.

It would be well if accumulated wealth were used in building projects for the benefit of the public. We visited various schools and missions and on Saturday, 5 January, we saw the young seventeen-year old boy King drive past with his attendants and retenue. Two days later, we met his royal yacht in the Persian Gulf.

Once more, our ship required more fuel oil. We docked long enough in Bahrein to get the supply tanks filled giving us enough time to walk on the docks which extend into the gulf.

After sailing along the coast of Iran for a day, we came to the Ormuz Straits and into the Gulf of Omar. The captain invited us to look through his binoculars at a very unique landmark formation on the rocky slopes of Iran.

At sunset, we were opposite the city of Yarsk and entered the Arabian Sea. The straight wake of the ship indicated that our bow was pointing straight towards Bombay.

Welcome back to India with flowers

Returning from Kodaikanal where I had placed our three youngest children in boarding, John and I prepared to tour the villages surrounding Mahbubnagar.

Touring was made easier because we now had a trailer. John fit a large wooden box-like structure with bunk beds, a folding table and a bench inside onto a truck chassis. A drop table was built on the outside of the trailer to facilitate dispensing medicine.

When we found a small hillock or a grove of trees a short distance away from the village, we would park the trailer. An enclosure of bamboo matting was set up for bathing and a hole dug for a latrine if the camp was to be in one place for several days.

This custom-built trailer was our home on long tours in the villages. It was hauled by our station wagon.

As soon as we stopped, crowds gathered for assistance. Those with sore eyes, boils, coughs, fevers, sprains and infections were very often also malnourished. I washed one poor child's eyes whose mother had put in chili pepper with boric acid water as a punishment. I then tried to soothe the child's excruciating pain with egg white spread on the eyes while giving the mother a stern talk about abusing her child.

John and the preachers walked to the nearby village to preach and visit homes. During this time, I met with the village women to study the Bible, sing and discuss preventive medicine, better diet and child care. The women were always eager to tell me their remedies: for example, what kinds of leaves to crush for the relief of insect bites; that cactus was good for boils and that tobacco leaves should be sprinkled under mats to discourage bedbugs.

Children played about and around us on the dry earth making objects with sticks and stones, chasing each other and squabbling. The women didn't mind how many children they had and worshiped the god of fertility. An extra child was not an extra mouth to feed but extra hands to work and to take care of the parents when they grew old.

After a full day and the evening meal, preachers and Bible women who had accompanied us gathered in an open area of the village around a lantern and started singing. It didn't take long before a large crowd gathered for an hour or more of speeches and songs. Occasionally, there were unpleasant incidents such as students remarking, "Look at all those pariah dogs," or "What a bunch of buffalos, they can't read or write but think they can understand what these *pari varu* (strange people) are saying."

Usually, however, we enjoyed the hospitality of the villagers and accepted invitations to meals and teas. Our camping equipment, customs and habits were a constant source of interest to villagers and their eyes followed all our movements until our lanterns were extinguished for the night.

The nights were short. Before dawn, women started their fires or gathered at the wells to draw water. Others went afield to relieve themselves. Children rose early to search for fuel or to fetch water and men coaxed oxen and animals to plow fields, pull loads and draw water for irrigation.

Our meals were cooked in a kettle set on three stones. When bystanders saw we were going to eat, they went away because they too didn't like to be watched while eating.

Visitors

Mahbubnagar was a District Headquarters with numerous offices where people had to come to obtain permits for rations, cars, and land dealings. Many who came for business transactions also visited John and me. School children, preachers, teachers, townspeople, priests and our own missionaries were in and out.

Travelers from different countries also came through Mahbubnagar. Some on motorcycles, some hitchhiking; some at wit's end, others willing to stay on for weeks and get advice as to further travel. World travelers, particularly western women, found it frustrating to hitchhike. Many of them wore brief attire and begged rides, behavior not acceptable for women in India. Many were critical of Indian behavior and culture without trying to understand it, a fact John and I discussed very often.

One guest was a wealthy man who came on a safari to hunt game. He had been staying in the grandest hotel in Hyderabad but was still disgruntled and generally unsympathetic with the local people. We tried to feed him foods he liked and took time to show him the work in and around Mahbubnagar. He eventually left to hunt tigers in North India after leaving a small donation for the school.

The Mosses, an Anglo-Indian couple, were regular visitors to our home and sometimes spent an entire evening. Mrs. May Moss was the aggressive one who loved good cuisine and conversation. Her bashful husband sat patiently and let her relate a story. When he turned in his chair or winced, we knew the tale was not the way he would have told it if he had the chance. Mrs. Moss produced her husband's teeth from her handbag at mealtime which caused our children much amusement. Mr. Moss was an administrative mechanic in the public works department (PWD) but seldom talked about himself although John tried again and again to coax him into discussions.

Hassan Ali Mirza, a respected advocate in Mahbubnagar, often visited us with his two wives. The older wife had only daughters so he married an attractive second wife who presented him with sons. The family sent a peon ahead to tell us they were coming so that no men would be present except for John.

As soon as the Mirzas entered, they removed their *burkahs* (veils) and opened their *pan dans* (bettlenut boxes). Small partitions in the stainless steel box held various aromatic spices and ingredients to be wrapped in a green leaf and chewed. We provided spittoons for them into which to spit the red juice.

Though we were not proficient in the Urdu language, we carried on a conversation with the help of Mr. Mirza who was conversant in English.

During the India-Pakistan partition, the Mirzas were not molested like other Muslims. However, Mr. Mirza was made to carry rocks from one pile to another for many days to humiliate him. Later, he was again recognized as a lawyer.

Our local District Superintendent of Police and District Collector were frequent visitors. The Collector came weekly to study German with us. He was interested in learning various languages, feeling sure he would be given a position in a foreign country before long. The Collector brought his French Bible, that someone had given him, and together with our German and Telugu Bibles, we studied the Gospel of John.

Kodaikanal School overlooking the lake

Social Life In Kodaikanal

We were exposed to little western culture on the plains and looked forward to Hill Season and programs arranged by the Highclerc School and community in Kodaikanal. Dramas ranging from "H.M.S. Pinafore" to "Tom Sawyer" were acted, as well as the Spring Concert given. Graduation exercises and sports events rounded out the activities. Those of us who had children participating in sports and band were also invited to the curry and rice feed on Benderloch Playing Field. The school cooks went out of their way to prepare delicious food and we enjoyed fine fellowship with other parents under the Eucalyptus trees.

Many missionaries were gifted in music, instrumental and voice; or in drama, speech or directing. Each year, after school functions were finished, parents practiced a cantata and a drama to be presented to the general public.

While these practices were going on, the annual "White Elephant Sale" was being organized. This was one of the highlights of the Hill Season. All who wanted to, brought used clothing and articles for sale. Each item was marked with a price and the owner's number. A part of the proceeds went to pay rental for the gymnasium in which the sale was held, a part to the school and the rest was realized by the seller.

The Industrial Sale was another important event. Salvation Army and other missions brought their crafts such as embroidery woven articles, clothing or foodstuffs for exhibit and sale. We often purchased our Christmas, anniversary and birthday gifts at this sale.

Mission groups took turns organizing a "tea" every Wednesday afternoon. "Specialties" of each group were served and thoroughly enjoyed.

After dramas and concerts, dinners at the KMU (Kodaikanal Mission Union) were also enjoyed. On some occasions, impromptu tap dancing on top of the tables by Dr. V. Rambo or a solo sung by L. Pickard were encored again and again.

The beautiful Palni Hills enticed us to enjoy many a hike or excursion to scenic places. Kodai Lake provided frequent delights for punting and boating. Various groups challenged each other to tennis and other sports. The Kodaikanal School Chapel, St. Peters Church and the Missouri Luthern Church were well attended on Sundays and during special events.

Most parents left Kodaikanal by 10 June for their work on the plains. So until next Hill Season . . .

IN APPRECIATION OF MY LOVELY FAMILY
"AUGUST JOY"

August Joy for me when on an August Morn
  I met my August heart's ease blooming.
I lost my heart to her but not to mourn
  She gave me hers for faithfully grooming.

August Joy when God's Celestial Firmament
  Released a Star (Esther) in all its loveliness
To lighten paths while in the Orient,
  For Christ to lighten unto Godliness.

August Joy when John our eldest son was born
  To gladen hearts and minds in parenthood.
His quests and answers always will adorn
  The memories of his charming days of boyhood.

August Joy when springtime April showers
  Sent to us related to the Lily of the Valley
The Violet (Viola Ruth) friendliest of all flowers
  That we should in His Garden round Him rally.

August Joy when peace which soothes and calms our lives,
  Was spoken of by Angels when they brought Irene.
Its peace when harmony in music thrives,
Its August peace that brings eternal joy serene.

August Joy when Paton heard the hearts of two,
  It was the longing of an August mother,
An August day brought David one of two,
  After the heart of God to live for one another.

August Joy at Midnight when we welcomed Paul
  To balance God's creation male and female.
August parents now are three and three who call
  Mama and Daddy with the love that will not fail.

August Joy on August Hills in extra measure
  When on a precipice was born another gift from heaven.
Her name: it's Marilyn coming out of God's eternal azure
  Completing God's perfection number seven.

August Joy when multiplied by nine,
  Joins all of us in lasting family ties.
August Joy far greater now than e'er before
  It lasts forever far above the tides.

Aug. 15
1954

Dedicated to my Beloved, Viola.
rev. John.
Happy Birthday!

The Mission Board gave John the responsibility to obtain the legal papers to start a medical center in Jadcherla. The site was on the highway to Hyderabad ten miles from Mahbubnagar.

With the help of workers, he tore down existing old walls of buildings which had been in ruins for many decades. Plans were made, together with Dr. and Mrs. Jake Friesen, to begin construction of a medical center.

One of the crucial problems at the new site was lack of water. Old wells, except for one a mile down from the area where the hospital was to be built, had run dry. Hauling water for construction and for making bricks was difficult.

Some missionaries and elders of the church gathered together with the construction workers. They knelt down in a circle and prayed to God for water. Arising from prayer John said, "Let us dig here." Though the villagers were skeptical, work was begun and a deep well was dug with prayer, faith and hard labor. It has never run dry.

The hundred-bed hospital was built and staffed and became known far and wide for excellent facilities, care, cleanliness, and capabilities of both foreign and Indian doctors and nurses. Nurses aid classes were started. Many girls got an opportunity to work and earn while they studied.

As the patient load grew, Dr. and Mrs. J. Froese, Dr. and Mrs. Bennett, and nurses, Regina Suderman, Frieda Newfeld, Joy Mercy Kelley and a dentist, Dr. and Mrs. J. Block joined Dr. and Mrs. J. Friesen. Workers' residences, nursing classrooms and a small chapel were built and landscaping done to improve the premises. A chaplain, chemist, technicians, drivers, repairmen, gardeners, cooks, matrons as well as male and female nurses contributed to the excellent medical facility.

The mission hospital has continued to function well under the able leadership of Dr. P.B. Arnold, superintendent, and his staff.

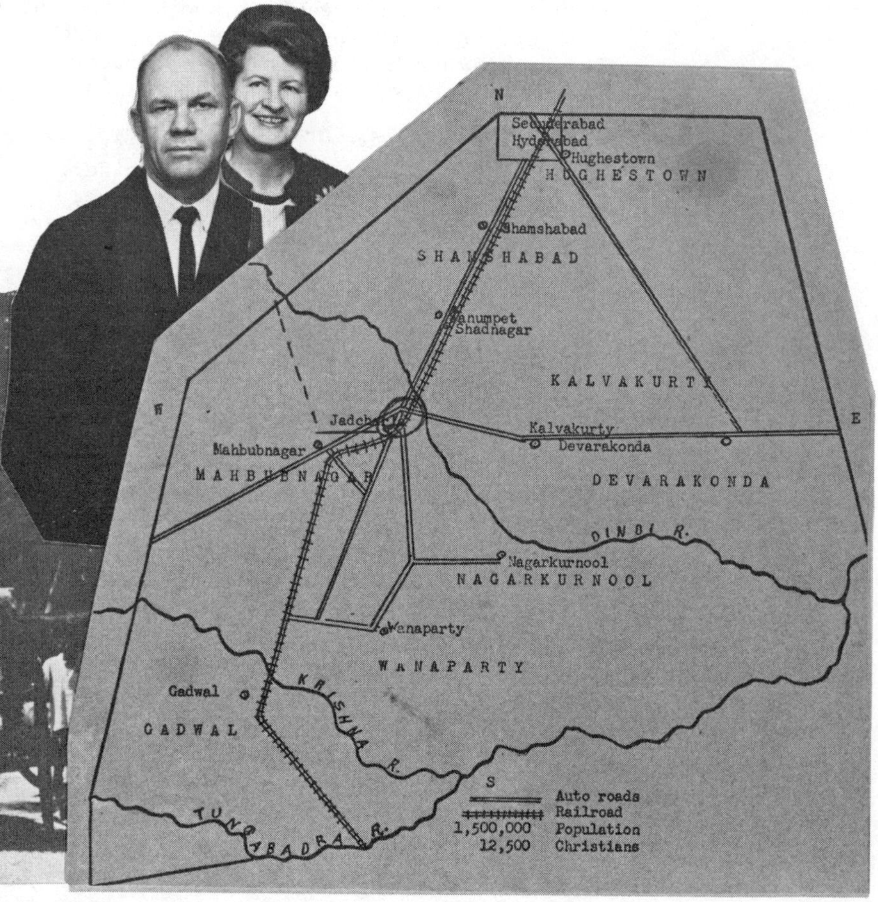

Dr. and Mrs. J. Friesen

Eyes blazing and hands shaking, one of the high school teachers came to John's office saying, "Sir, I wish you to expel Parvathi at once."

"Sit down," John said, "Tell me what upsets you so."

The teacher's voice shook with emotion. "It's this way, sir, Parvathi has been to a *sode cheppe amma* (witch) living near the railway station to get a potion to put into my food so I will love her. Please dismiss her before she plays tricks with me or I will leave the school."

After praying and talking with the teacher John promised to look into the matter further. He asked me to find out what I could at the girls' boarding.

Calling Parvathi and the matron, Gnanamma, I heard the girl's story: "I wanted the teacher to take notice of me, for he never did, so I consulted one who could make a good prediction to help me."

"Where did you go and who gave you money for this?" I asked.

"I told the matron I wanted to visit relatives in my village. The cost was very little. I had a few rupees and Chensamma was satisfied."

Gnanamma was curious as to what the woman had given Parvathi as a potion. "She gave me this," Parvathi said holding up a bottle of what looked like a mixture of spices. "She told me to watch where the teacher walked, then to take a little dust from his footprint. I was to mix this dust with the mixture she made for me into chicken curry I prepared and serve it to the teacher," Parvathi explained.

The matron who had sat quietly, suddenly burst out with "You are a *chedda pilla* (naughty girl) and you a Christian at that."

Sending a message with a man by railway to Gadwal, we asked Parvathi's parents to come and discuss the matter with us. Their decision was to take their daughter back to Gadwal where they would try and find a husband for her.

The teacher, still distraught, refused to attend classes until Parvathi left the school, fearful that she would cast an evil spell on him.

More and more children were sent to mission boarding schools. Fees were low. Ten to fifteen rupees per month per child for tuition, food and books. On 4 October 1955, John was quoted in a newspaper article as stating that 380 children were enrolled in school. Rs. 1650, close to $400, was paid to sixteen qualified teachers. Over one-half of this was paid by the Government of India in the form of Grant-in-aid.

The government also gave generous sums for worthy Christian and non-Christian students. Students who generally needed the assistance were *Harijans* (formerly outcaste). Most of the day scholars came from the upper castes. Our school's reputation for qualified instruction and good discipline encouraged more and more officials to enroll their children.

The District Collector of Mahbubnagar District had two very bright sons in school. When the final yearly examinations for high school were given, the Collector asked that the younger eleven-year old be allowed to sit for the same exams his older brother was taking. John obtained permission from the State Board and the boy passed with honors.

The District Collector in the center, his eleven-year old son mentioned above, on the right near John, and two other sons

John's Hall, named after son John who contributed some of his first earnings for the hostel, provided the boys with running tap water in their own kitchen and nice quarters in which to live.

Shanti Bhavan, the hostel for the girls, was filled to capacity. About one hundred girls had their own well for water, bathrooms and a garden area. Surrounding the dormitory was a wall with a gate opening into the larger school compound.

The older girls in the boarding helped Laxamma, a woman hired to supervise and do the cooking and clean the grain, vegetables and lentils. The older boys pounded the grain and chopped firewood.

Milo and a hot curry sauce made of lentils or vegetables was served to the school boarders twice a day. The large school garden, which the children helped to weed and water, yielded tomatoes, okra, eggplant and greens for the boarders' meals. Rice was served twice a week and meat was served only occasionally.

Outsiders called the mission school children *sankati pillalu* (kaffir corn children) partly with jest, partly with envy, for the mission school won prize after prize in competitive sports. We were able to influence others concerning good nutrition and better stamina.

The boarders slept on locally made mats spread on the stone floors. During the cool season, their thin blankets were not adequate to keep them warm. Colds were common and infectious diseases spread rapidly from one to the other. If the children were too ill to visit my clinic, I took them medicine and injections on evening rounds, always accompanied by my black cat which was a faithful companion. Very sick children were taken to our central medical hospital or Dr. J. Friesen from Jadcherla came to visit them. We received Rs. 50, about $16 per year for medication, which only paid for aspirin and Epson salts. Other medication was purchased with donations from friends or relatives.

In order to obtain the staples such as rice, flour and *jowar* (millet) in large quantities for the school, John had to spend many hours at ration offices in Hyderabad City in order to get permits.

John spent all morning in one office waiting to see the officer in charge without success. Most of the staff left the building at noon, but John stayed sitting on the verandah. He had accounts and other books to look at and waited until the people returned from lunch. Seeing him seated there, they inquired, "Have you had your food?"

"No, I am waiting here for my ration papers," was his reply.

"You can go now and come back tomorrow," the peon suggested.

Knowing tomorrow never comes, John waited on. It was nearly closing time and John was tired and hungry. Doors were being closed and bolted. The chief officer exclaimed when he walked past John, "I didn't know you were still here!" "But I am," John said, "and have come a long distance."

Indian courtesy came to John's aid and the officer said, "*Chipprase* (peon), open the door and get the Sahib's papers."

In less than five minutes, the papers were stamped, signed, *salaams* (greetings) said and John proceeded to the guest house for the night.

For several years, the Church World Service donated large quantities of beans, milk powder, butter oil and cheese. At first, the boarding children did not like the beans but we persisted and added chilies and onions to make the beans more palatable. Cheese, likewise, was unfamiliar to the boarders, but later became a favorite snack.

Milk powder was mixed with water in five gallon tins every weekday evening by some volunteers. Children from the locality were invited and sat down in rows. The mixed milk was served to them in mugs or whatever containers they brought.

Some of the children were persuaded by their elders to bring their portion of milk outside the compound walls and sell it or give it to "sweet merchants" and then come back for more. Thereafter, we insisted the children drink the milk in our presence.

At Deepavali, the Festival of Lights, our Mahbubnagar Collector wrote us requesting several gallon tins of butter oil to light his lamps for the festival.

If we refused, it might have meant that our permits to remain in India would be rejected. John and I thought about it and replied, "This oil is sent for the poor and we are not permitted to give it to anyone for purposes other than cooking."

We waited a little apprehensively for his response. A peon, sent by the Collector a few days later, came with a letter stating: "I appreciate your honesty and openness in refusing the oil I requested. I do understand your position. Please carry on with the philanthropic work for our Indian people."

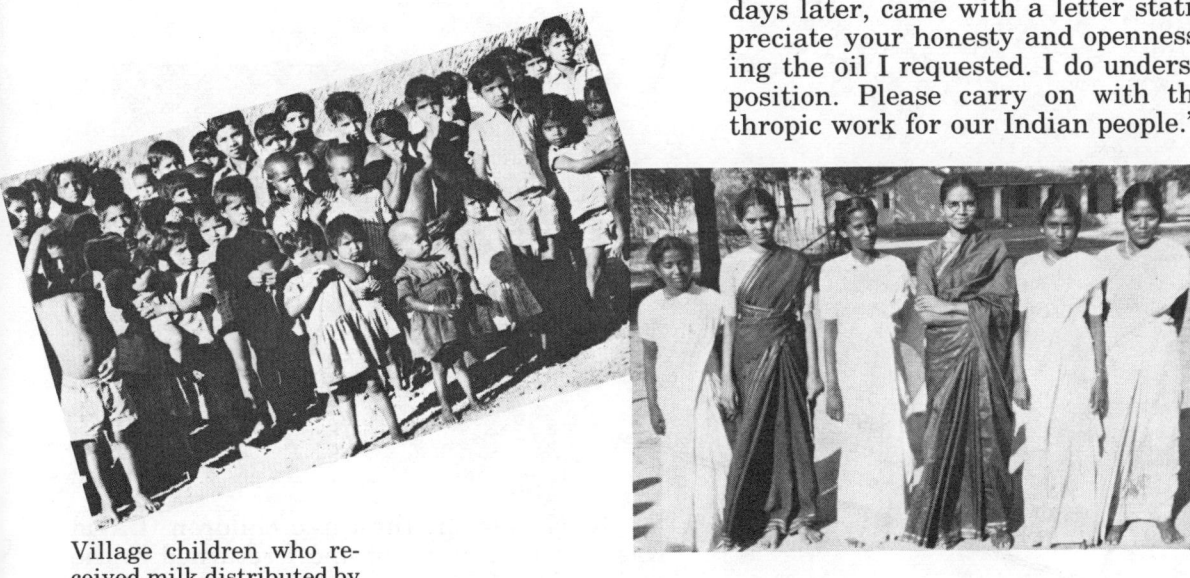

Village children who received milk distributed by teachers who volunteered their services

In March of 1954, our son David's back gave him much trouble and it was thought that he had hurt it while pole-vaulting. Later, however, an X-ray showed that he had tuberculosis of the spine and needed traction and bed rest for months. Dr. Thomas provided medical expertise and I nursed David and stayed with the three youngest children in Kodaikanal from May until November while John returned to the plains.

I missed John, but we corresponded frequently.

John addressed his letters to me "his own" in various ways.

"Precious family on the hilltop," "....."Have just bathed from bald to soles."

"Heart's own," "....."This is a big house. I would like to make it into a school room but must not do it without sanction."..

"Darling Viola. Your name stands for music, flowers, painting and femininity."

"Sweet Violet with seven lovely petals," "Glad you are the same sweet girl despite a broken fibula bone. I do still want you to run several races with me, so please keep that pretty leg up."

"My happy Pairs among the Pears," Lush. I had noodles with brown onions over and vinegar trickling through to make them slide into the many feet of digestive system."

"My Dear Viola," "People begin to talk about the Maha Sabha (a smaller political party in India) agitating with "missionaries get out." So far it is not a very weighty matter but we never know how far they will go and what the final results will be. Here all is quiet People in the compound and village are helpful and understanding."

"Darling," "You are now dreaming of me. I am typing on the portable, comes to mind: I have a portable heart and so can be with you tonight! Wonderful. While walking from dining to office room, I met a scorpion and you can guess the rest. Samadhanama will wonder how the smear got on the floor when she washes tomorrow."

In November, the three children (David was in a cast by then) and I returned to the plains. The Ghul Mohar, *Vepa* and Frangipani trees were abloom. Seventeen varieties of roses welcomed us back to Mahbubnagar for the Christmas holidays.

"Beloved M-Squared,"

"It is so hot this year. I must admit I feel like Nehru said, "stale." I have a brighter bulb in the bathroom now and an surprised I did not think of it sooner. I go there to read and to be quiet. Yesterday, I picked up one of Mama's magazines. A picture of my breakfast plate with two fried eggs with brown hash and a teaspoon of mama's purple jam as near the eggs as possible with tea steaming close by, would send many Americans to Mahbubnagar. I think it would. The sad thing is my, our Indian people do not see much of it. However, there is comfort in this: rice is cheaper and they can top this with steaming hot "pappu."

"In this magazine I also read that Colgate's brings the sweetheart. I have now bought two tubes of Colgates to see whether she will come. However, I am very happy that the children have more time with their Mama who is preparing them for life's separation......"

Thank you for letters!

..... Daddy

"Beloved,"

"It is so dark. Heavy clouds hanging low after a moist night. I just called to one guy to quit breaking down branches to get the flowers. Why can't people work with a little forethought? It's all "hand to mouth." For today with no thought for tomorrow.

"The conference? Well Viola, you would not want me to write all the hollow things and of that there was so much. I sat in front of the chairman "Dick Tator" and helped where I could. The highschool reports were accepted without thanks. Treasury reports oked with ovation. Bruton accounts approved without appreciation. HSC reports listened to with disdain and some snickering.
The garden was my "retreat"......"

"Darling and darlings in the Hill Nest,"
"I am sleepy. I love you and should say much more but I will dream so hard that you will dream it all in. Be sure you do not forget to pull over the blankets before you sleep. Also close the kitchen door. Did you all brush your teeth? Nipper lies at the door. The cinemas howl in the distance.
Night, night.   Your John, Daddy"

Little did people in the homeland realize how yearningly we looked forward to correspondence. We blessed those who wrote frequently and kept us informed.

Before airmail, letters took at least a month and often two to arrive. When our daughter, Esther, was born, John's parents in America received the announcement one day later by cable. My parents, who lived in India, received the news one week later!

Dr. J. Friesen, who was cabled of his father's death while on the high seas en route to India, had to wait another two months after reaching the subcontinent, before he received details of the death.

Arriving one midnight at missionary J. Voths, we found them pouring over letters from their children which had been delivered at sundown. Their faces were aglow as they said, "We have just received letters from our children and friends and now have enough money and encouragement to continue."

> Received my new dress today — by mail. It's nice.
>
> Thanks to Marilyn, David, & Paul for your encouraging letters.
>
> Feels good to have you say Come!!

Chits (notes) were sent with a peon (messenger) to announce special events and ask people for meals. An announcement of a meeting to be held or cancelled was taken by someone on a bicycle or by bus.

Children in boarding schools learnt early to write weekly letters starting with "I am well and happy, I hope you are the same," until content and form developed into newsy informative letters. At one juncture, a weekly letter from Kodaikanal had not arrived, but a delayed telegram came saying," Viola Ruth dangerously ill, come at once."

Sending a runner to our parents in Nagarkurnool to come and stay with our youngest three, we took a bus to the railroad station, boarded a train, then again a bus up the ghat to Kodaikanal. As we slowly crawled up the road, we passed the cemetery where a grave was being dug. "Is that for our daughter?" we wondered. A few minutes on up the road, the bus turned into the boarding where our children stayed. One of the teachers, seeing us, rushed out with the glad news, "Ruthie is much better."

In closing we would like to encourage all of you to write. We all are very busy but not too busy to write a little note to the Wiebes in India. Your letters are a definite encouragement while in the work on the missionfield.

Money was always a problem. There was never enough cash. Sometimes salaries arrived late or there was simply not enough to make ends meet.

John encouraged village preachers to try to manage on their *bata* (allowance) even though it was not enough. Land disputes, court cases, school, church and compound building and maintenance consumed more finances than we had access to despite money gifts from friends and relatives.

The following are some excerpts from some of John's letters:

... "I sent you another Rs. 100/- I was able to dig up. Money is still on the other side of the Atlantic and Pacific for that matter. Maybe it sank and money still is heavier than the ocean. Today good old Sangaya agreed to give me Rs. 1000/0 loan so I am running the show again saving where I can. Started on press work again today. I must send you (Viola) some of this money. Surely the big sums we expect and anticipate must come or the Mennonites will need to close the gate to Hillsboro. Maybe it has been "Hills" so long that now we are shifting to the second half of the name "Boro" spelling it "borrow." I should not say these things. We must pray more."

... "I am awfully sorry you are short of money (Viola). Terrible. Don't tell the children, but no money has come yet for September and October. Our Board is not in a position to send it seemingly. Your letter took me to the Post Office this morning and I sent some money by express money order. Pay only the most needed things please. The school and merchants can wait. I'll send you money when I can lay hold of it. Your John."

"Pennyless bosses have little to say."

You may now draw up to 700 in cheques. I am sending blanks. Will you take care of your immediate needs, tell you come? I am writing in P.O. Must now run. Love, John

John, in an address to his colleagues wrote: "We and our Indian brothers and sisters often look for clouds of rain. We also look to bags in the safe but if we for one moment stop to think of how many of our Indian colleagues depend on showers from heaven and how very few depend on the mission 'safe,' we would pray oftener for showers.

"On the Mahbubnagar field, Christians number about 700. If we calculate Rs. four per month per person, it would come to Rs. forty-eight a year. 700 Christians would require Rs. 33,600 per year. But our total appropriations for the station, making extra allowances for other gifts, means only about Rs. 6000. Therefore, for our Christians alone, Rs. 27,600 must annually be granted by our Heavenly Father by sending showers of rain and letting the earth produce."

"Complete confusion prevailed in this town of over 20,000 population," John wrote in a newspaper article.

"Word had spread that the bank of the Mahbubnagar City water supply reservoir was giving way and that a flood was threatening a large part of the town including the mission compound. Warned by fleeing bypassers, we hurried to higher ground with the school boarders where we were informed much to our relief that it was a false alarm. Before midnight, all was quiet."

It was late afternoon and terribly hot. The earth was parched, the trees yellowing; not a leaf stirred. Only the brain fever birds interrupted the tense quiet before the ensuing storm.

Like a massive wall, the heavy black clouds rolled in from the east. Then a single crack of thunder and the smell of wet earth preceded the sheets of rain. Like a locomotive, the roar of wind and rain bore down on masses of people huddled together in their flimsy huts. With fear and dread, they prayed the *tupannu* (heavy wind) would not vent its fury on their village. Their fate was sealed however, as a huge tidal wall of water washed inland several kilometers, inundating the entire village, tearing at mud walls, drowning livestock and chickens, uprooting the trees, engulfing the people and washing them out to sea.

Another mountainous wave followed the first and tore away the remains of the houses. With it, some of the bodies taken out by the first wave, were hurled back on shore only to be taken back to their watery graves. Many bodies were sighted days later miles down the beach. All except a baby and five teenage boys died in one village.

On one of the rafters of a mud house which had collapsed, a mother had tied a basket in which she laid her small baby. The basket, miraculously, floated free of the debris and rafters and drifted inland to high ground.

After the storm, people from another village came to see the damage. They saw a large cobra uncoil itself from outside a basket and slither away. Looking into the basket, they found a whimpering naked baby boy with only a string tied about his waist. "He must have belonged to wealthy caste people," those who saw him remarked because he was wearing gold anklets. One of the men offered to take the little child home to his wife and bring him up as his own.

CENTRAL RAILWAY

OFFICE OF THE
DIVISIONAL SUPERINTENDENT,
SECUNDERABAD-DECCAN.
Camp: Mahbubnagar.
Dated 13-9-56.

No.

Dear Rev. Wiebe,

You are probably aware that through communication between Mahbubnagar and Secunderabad was restored last night and we hope to return to-day to Secunderabad for pursuing our enquiry there. Before I leave, I should like to thank you and Mrs. Wiebe most sincerely for all the interest taken and assistance which you extended to our workers at the site of accident. The generous gift of milk and cheese was greatly appreciated. We shall always look back with pleasant recollections of the kindness shown by all our friends at Mahbubnagar during our period of trial.

Thanking you once again.

(R. Hydari)

Rev. Wiebe,
Menonite Mission,
Mahbubnagar.

INDIA
JOHN A WIEBE WRITES
The Mahbubnagar Railroad Accident 121 Lives Lost
September 1, 1956

Viola and I are writing this on a Sunday. Just a week after the very very tragic accident happened. A passenger train, engine and nine cars made its way around a curve near the little village of Appanpalli when, due to heavy cloud bursts, it plunged into turbulant waters. It happened at 12:40 at night. Over a hundred lives were lost.

Crowds and crowds (India can have bigger crowds than any other land) were moving towards the scene of accident. After winding our way through anxious masses we arrived at the stream which had become a wide river. Nearing the damaged road bridge we viewed with sad feelings the bodies of many dead. Old and young and children even babies. An accident is no respector of persons. The poor and the rich died together

in muddy and violent waters. The complete top of one of the railroad cars was carried to the farther side of the highway a mile downstream from the place of accident. Trees along the side of the stream were either uprooted or bent completely over by the force of the deluge. Clothes and belongings of the dead were dangling from branches and shrubs. While crossing the badly damaged bridge it was shocking to look downstreams which was lined with dead. The engine was leaning precariously off the farther bank at a slope. It had smashed right through the wide pillars supporting the thirty foot girders Earth behind the pillars had been eroded by the fast running torrents. Six cars were still standing on the tracks. In front of these a first and second class car was leaning over into the rushing and foaming stream with the farther end completely crushed to splinters. The two third class cars which spilt their passengers into the water had been demolished and crushed between the engine and oncoming cars. Such cars have a capacity for 70 passengers on meter guage trains and invariably carry many more passengers

October 1955

"----- It was a beautiful sunny day when we set out for the Kurmurti Jatra (fair) where once a year the Hindus of this area got to bathe in the "holy" pool on the hill.

The distance was thirty miles on a rutted dirt road. On the way we passed hundreds of pilgrims on foot or on ox-carts, carrying their possessions in sacks. Every hardship, inconvenience and trial was endured without a murmur. The lame, the blind, the lepers, the majority too poor to buy a change of clothing, jostling, chattering, spitting, sweating.

John and I were a gazing stock to them --- standing in the hot sun, speaking to those who cared to listen, doling out medicines on the dusty way side.

---- As the darkness fell, we hurriedly pitched camp, ate supper, and went to the village to meet with the Christians in their "palem". (area)

----- Early next morning we were awakened by the clang of bells and the shouting of "Sita-Rama" (Hindu dieties) as hundreds hurried to the pool to wash away their sins ---

---- The following day we passed a group who had been at the jatra for several days, and asked them, "What have you received?" To this they replied, "Shanti leka potimi, Shanti leka vastimi". We went without peace, we return without peace" ----

The Jubilee Road wound through a teakwood tree reserve. This was an unpopulated area covered with small trees and shrubs. A quiet stream flowed next to our favorite picnic site, a place we visited frequently when the children were home from school. Panthers roamed the hills and small wildlife was apparent although it was quickly disappearing because of the poaching and hunting.

Bird life was abundant with now and then brilliant color among the shrubs. We stopped to allow a group of Lombardis to pass. The women wearing appliqued, brightly colored full skirts swung towards us, pausing to chat. Their men, drab by comparison, stood behind.

"Where are you going?" we asked one particularly striking woman. "To the *cheetapalla pandlu* trees and then to weed the milo while the men channel the water."

Cheetapalla pandlu was said to have been derived from *Sita ballapu pandlu* (the fruit that the goddess Sita wanted on her table). It was the delicious custard apple that grew wild in the hills. The Lombardis picked baskets of the fruit and sold them in the marketplace.

"Where are your children?" we asked.

"They are near our houses with their grandmothers," they said, pointing towards the thatched huts surrounded by trees, some distance from the road.

"When will you go home?"

"Oh, when the sun is there," one remarked pointing to the west.

"Will the *avvalu* make the evening meal before you get home?"

"Most of us bring home peppers and onions and we will cook. Perhaps the children will have gathered twigs for the fire and cleaned the *jannalu* (milo) so we can make *rottelu* (flat bread)."

"What do you do after you eat?"

"Usually we are too tired. We nurse our babies, then sleep on our *tzaapalu* (mats)."

"Do you sometimes dance?" we asked hoping that they would sing and dance for us.

Ah ah. Yarre-Eh-Yarre-Eh and they began slow rhythmic turns, dancing in a circle and chanting in their language, bracelets and anklets jangling. Their men smiled, amused with our appreciation for their women.

When the women completed a few turns, they stretched out their hands asking for money. Patting their stomachs, they said they would put what they purchased with it there.

Another day, driving along the road, we met a young woman wailing plaintively, swirling in slow circles in her new garments. An older woman followed and quite a distance behind her came a young man dressed in a clean *dhoti* (loin cloth) white shirt and turban wrapped around his head.

We stopped and inquired as to why the woman was wailing. "She is to be married," the old woman said, "and has to show her sorrow in leaving home."

Lombardi women wrap themselves, jewelry mirrored garments and all, in a shawl at night. Their intricately embroidered mirror work could be ruined with washing so their clothing is not cleaned often. During our time in Andhra Pradesh, when a woman of this tribe died, the jewelry from her neck, arms and ankles was removed and left under a tree. Then the entire community moved but always stayed near the fields.

Always neatly attired, Y. Rueben worked as a foreman in the mission printing press. He had a nice wife and family. They lived in one of the better dwellings with a private well in an adjoining compound where they could also grow a small garden.

During the Hill Season while John and I were absent, Rueben, who was competent, was left in charge of supervising the mission compound activities. One year, upon our return to the plains, we were upset to hear that Rueben and Krupadanam, a teacher, had been found guilty of sexually misusing a young orphan girl. Mary had been abandoned and was found sleeping with the buffalo. The villagers brought her to John and me, and we arranged for and financed her upkeep with an elderly woman who lived on the compound and acted as Mary's guardian.

Both Rueben and Krupadanam were dismissed from their jobs. Rueben, the press foreman, was so incensed at losing his position that he brought a lawsuit against John and the mission. A veterinarian friend and a government officer lent Rueben large sums of money to fund the case.

The court case dragged on for months. Every morning, a peon from the court summoned the plaintiff and the defendant to appear at a certain hour. John arrived promptly only to wait for hours on a hard bench in the heat sitting under an antiquated, slowly rotating fan before being called into the small courtroom where he and a few others heard the accusations.

The mission employed an advocate for Rs. 770 (about $250) who did what he could to help. Persons who were called to witness were sometimes fearful to tell the truth because of possible reprisals.

Finally, ten months later, the gruelling court case was over. John was exonerated and Rueben was told to leave his quarters on the mission compound.

The veterinarian doctor who had funded Rueben's case died unexpectedly some months later. His funeral was conducted in the church cemetery and John gave the message. The District Collector and others who heard John said that his words, as nothing else, had spoken to them of Christian forgiveness.

Mary, the orphan, was sent to a school for unwed mothers in another district where she learned a trade in order to support herself and her child.

A bright young Hindu boy by the name of Sri Hari regularly attended the Bible class I taught in high school. He asked intelligent questions but was often cynical and disruptive, so much so that sometimes I found it difficult to teach because he antagonized the other students into unruly conduct.

One day he did not attend classes but came and announced, "I am going to be trained by the army and when I come back, I will burn down the Christian churches and schools and drive away all the foreigners."

Soon after this, Sri Hari and some of his friends took heavy sticks and entered the back of the church during a service. People became restless and talked among themselves. John, troubled by the disturbance, dismissed the congregation with a short prayer. Directing the school girls back to their hostel, we told them to stay indoors. The District Superintendent of Police was told about the disorderly conduct and he sent policemen to guard the compound for a few days. No further incident occurred.

Some years later, a young man in uniform appeared as I was dispensing medicine to the school boarders. He saluted me and asked whether I remembered him. When I said I didn't, he said, "I am Sri Hari and I have come to apologize and to say I now appreciate what you are doing."

I shook his hand and praised the Lord.

Kodaikanal School graduation exercises were well attended by parents and other vacationing missionaries. In 1956, our twins graduated and John, their Father, was the commencement speaker.

David and Paul, together with their classmates, then left for America, traveling back through Europe, reaching their respective colleges in time for the fall term.

A month after reaching Hillsboro, the twins ushered at the wedding of daughter Irene to Donovan Janzen. Viola Ruth and Herbert Friesen now lived in Greeley, Colorado, and son John and his wife, Carol (Hiebert), lived in Thousand Oakes, California. Esther was completing her nursing course in Denver, Colorado.

Traveling third class, John, Marilyn and I went by train to North India in May. The trip was hot and crowded, but interesting. Winding up the *ghat* in a small cog-train, we thoroughly enjoyed the change and the beauty of the hill station, Darjeeling. Enjoying the high altitude sun, we walked up and down the lovely hillsides and along a mountain path viewing the splendor of the Katchenjanga Mountain Range. A screen of pink clouds moved aside to allow a glimpse of Mt. Everest from Tiger Hill very early one morning.

As we walked along the narrow cobble streets, we saw a friendly lady wearing an apron over her long striped skirt. She was standing outside the house next to a plaque on which was written "Norkay TenSing." We greeted the smiling lady. Mrs. TenSing, whom she introduced herself as, invited us into their immaculate little home for tea. We were soon joined by Norkay TenSing who, with Hillary, had climbed Mt. Everest.

All too soon, we had to leave for the plains. In Patna, Bihar, we were to board a plane for Katmandu, Nepal. It was a stifling 120 degrees. Nothing stirred during midday. We found relief by wrapping wet sheets around our bodies and sitting under an overhead fan in our small guest house. Towards evening, people began to stir, venturing out onto the dusty streets to buy and sell their wares.

The next day, we boarded a creaking bus for the airport. We were advised to get there early, as each person had to be weighed along with his or her luggage. Some people decided to remain behind with their heavy tin trunks hoping to take the flight the following day. Extra weight, the pilot said, would endanger the small craft flying over vast mountain ranges.

We reached Katmandu, the capital of Nepal, misty with rain and bright with flowers, after a very bumpy flight. There we rejoiced to meet with our children, Herbert and Ruth Friesen and their small son Stanley, the first grandson with whom we became acquainted. Herbert was serving as the General Surgeon in the Christian Hospital made famous by Dr. B. Flaming and her ornithologist husband. The former king of Nepal's palace had been renovated as a hospital to serve the people.

Our children lived in part of another renovated palace not far away. There Ruth introduced us to water buffalo meat made palatable when tenderized with papaya and disguised with spices.

The paths from one place to another were lined with gardenia hedges. Creepers climbed over the rocks and walls. Herb and Ruth took time to accompany us through picturesque streets around the Stupa. There we watched people touching and spinning the prayer wheels as they passed. The great eyes painted on the Stupa watched the throngs below.

After two weeks, we parted from our children and traveled back by bus and train to the plains of Hyderabad and Mahbubnagar.

Mount Everest and Norkay TenSing

The church in the mission compound of Mahbubnagar had been built at the turn of the century. The cement roof, supported by long heavy iron beams placed on mud walls, was beginning to show wear. Big cracks in the walls had been plastered again and again and could not withstand too many more heavy winds and monsoon rains.

Local members were opposed to building a church in another location as the present site was considered "holy ground," and had been built by the beloved Dr. E. Chute. "This is where we have always worshiped and where we will continue to worship," the people said.

The rains came down heavily at 4:00 a.m. one morning. With a huge crash, the roof of the church caved in, bending the iron girders and causing the building to collapse. Had this happened a few hours earlier, many communicants would have been crushed to death.

Despite continued opposition, the foundation for a new church was dug and built on higher ground of an unused section of the compound. John had the damaged old church building repaired and sectioned off into classrooms for the growing school. We continued to use the building for our church meetings.

Construction of the new church commenced slowly as funds donated by friends came in.

The day the cornerstone was to be laid came. The event had been publicized and everyone invited to attend. Pastor M.B. John and Balliah, the mason, came, then John and I arrived. The four of us waited and waited. No one else came. Clearly people were demonstrating their opposition to building a new sanctuary. We were crushed, but we read the Word together, prayed and committed the House of God to His Glory and John laid the cornerstone.

Pastor M.B. John at the left, and visiting dignitaries and speakers at the dedication

M. Balliah, small in stature, an expert in mason work, was faithful to the end. He stood tall and smiling at the dedication.

Funds were slow in arriving but we continued praying. One day, we received $1000 from Sara, Katherine and Suzie Balzer. It was an answer to prayer. The money had been donated to mission work by their brother who died suddenly. John was now able to hire laborers. Walls went up with locally made bricks. Window and door frames were inserted and an asbestos roof laid. A tower with an open cross on four sides completed the House of Prayer.

Clouds formed a "Shekinah Cloud of Glory," a portent of God's presence, above the church tower the day we dedicated the sanctuary. Several Mennonite Brethren, including Rev. J.B. Toews, arrived from America. The District Collector, District Superintendent of Police, missionaries and crowds of local residents who had been in opposition to building a new church, now crowded to get into the sanctuary on 28 July 1957.

A bell donated by the Mahbubnagar Women's Mission Group under the leadership of Mrs. M. Krupamma John, was ordered from the foundry in southern India and hung in the tower. On dedication day, the bell tolled and we rejoiced.

Radio Work

We held meetings in the large village of Ippakunta. John and the preachers spoke, and Telugu hymns were sung accompanied by men playing *tabalas* (drums). One evening the *pujari* (priestess) called two preachers, John and me to her home.

We left our shoes at the door and entered the dim room, refusing her offer of *chai* (tea) but sitting with her on mats she spread on the dirt floor. Pointing to some niches carved into the walls, she said, "Please take those *bommalu* (idols) you see there and throw them into the well. I have been hearing you speak and have heard the same words on the radio many times. I want to get rid of them."

John replied, "Amma, we are not the ones who have worshiped the idols. You will have to take them and throw them away."

"I?" she questioned with a shudder, but she gathered the two or three idols in a basket and we went outside. Walking hurriedly two or three hundred yards to the well, she threw the basket and contents into it. A few curious children peered into the dark depths but the water had already enveloped the idols.

Perhaps fearing that she would be struck dead or that fire would come from the heavens, the priestess looked at us. We led her quietly back to her house where we sat and prayed together, encouraging her with words of hope.

Click, click. Radios were switched on for the seven o'clock "God has spoken ministries" of R.R.K. Murty and Henry Poetker, aired via medium wave on a 400,000 watt station from Ceylon (now Sri Lanka). The program was strong enough to be heard in practically every corner of India.

Lively music by young Christian people and the gospel message was beamed forth. The impact of the radio ministry was seen in the "houses of prayer" which were started in many villages where most of the Christians were illiterate and there was no preacher.

Henry Poetker wrote (16 Jan. 1981, Herald), "Even though only 3.4 per cent of the population is Christian, the Christian gospel appears to have great appeal."

Mennonite Brethren have been involved in radio work since the 1950s. Students from Mahbubnagar High School and Pastor John and teacher, Bhagavandos, went with John to Jadcherla once a week to record on Dr. J. Friesen's tapes. These were then sent to Ceylon to be put on radio.

Preachers, teachers and Bible women at a seminar held in Mahbubnagar to promote the Laubach method. Rev. John Wesley, sitting on my left, and other educators.

Dr. Laubach, for whom the adult literacy program is named, developed the picture alphabet method for many languages.

Telugu has thirty-nine consonants and thirteen subscribed letters for which to find pictures. The charts are clear and teachers enjoyed teaching this method. Illiterate people found the picture alphabet easy to understand. Villagers first drew their letter in the sand, later slates were used until the students graduated to pencil and paper.

Farewell Address Presentented To
Rev. & Mrs. John A. Wiebe.

Sir and Madam,

We, the staff and students of the Mennonite Brethren Central High School propose to present you with this farewell address on the eve of your departure home after strenuous service for nearly 32 years in this alien soil having come over here in 1927 leaving your home-land for service in this distant area thousands of miles away from your mother country. This bespeaks to your missionary zeal, courage and enterprise imbued with devotional service to God.

We have learnt with great pride that your service in the early years in the peri – pheri area of Mahbubnagar, such as Deverkonda, Nagarkurnool, Kalwakurthy and Janampet found recognition at the hands of the mission as evidenced by your promotion as the missionary-in-charge of the head-quarters at Mahbubnagar, and where you have trudged through successfully in piloting the institution between the years 1937 to 1946.

You have been in our midst during the years 1952—1959 as principal of the High School. Your presence was warmly felt by every one of your students and also the staff attached to the institution of which you have been the head.

The activities of the school were sufficiently enlarged by you. The boys' hostel, the teachers' quarters, the printing press, the ladies quarters and the primary school, all these annexures to the High School are monumental of your solid work at this end, not to speak or eulogise your services rendered in conducting regular Church services, Bible classes and distribution of medicines and milk food to the poor and needy.

Your characteristic smile and pleasing behaviour and amiable manners to the students and staff have always shed a benificient influence on those that came into contact with you. There is nothing which you did not touch without adorning it.

Please accept our hearty felicitations for a safe "bon-voyage" to you and to Mrs. Wiebe. We pray for a long and prosperous life to you both.

The staff and students of the M. B. C. High School, Mahbubnagar, India.

March 19, 1959.

Festive occasions and programs in India involved many days of preparation. Giant *pandals* (canvas or mat spreads) were strung from poles dug into the ground to cover the participants. Chairs and benches were placed on a portable wooden stage for the VIPs (Very Important Persons) and speakers. The audience sat on mats on the ground under the shade of the *pandal*.

Protocol was important and guests were seated accordingly. Speeches welcoming the guests were given and garlands of roses or marigolds and jasmin were placed around the necks of the chief guests. Eloquent speakers paid particular attention to details, sometimes rambling on for thirty minutes.

If it was a farewell, a framed statement glowing with compliments and achievements pertaining to the person(s) was presented. More speeches followed. Programs often lasted two or three hours. If anyone of us demured that "We can't have such a long program," the response was inevitably "We want the occasion to be worthwhile."

The Christian *Kalaksheypam* is the story of a Bible character told in drama and song. The lead character, accompanied by drums, started with a catchy phrase depicting a chapter of the Bible which was to follow. Persons standing on either side of the leader chanted *Sandanna, Sandanna* rhythmically together with drums to emphasize the phrase. Similarly, King David in writing the Psalms said "Selah."

Most of the crowd, no matter how long the *Kalaksheypam* lasted, sat with rapt attention. Part of the audience dozed but were sure to wake up at least to hear the grand climax. John and I usually retired long before the drama was half over to dream our own *sandannas*. Some missionaries became quite proficient in performing this type of storytelling.

Rev. B.A. Masalamani an often invited guest speaker (top center, below right)

Degrees, certificates, credentials, merit plaques were framed and decorated the walls of offices and homes of those who earned them.

It was prestigious to flaunt one's accomplishments. Even if one failed a degree, the attempt was mentioned:
Mr. Samuel Rao
BA Pass
MA failed
During an interview with John, a man was asked about his achievements and replied, "I have an FA."

"What does FA represent?" John asked.

"Well," was his response, "I tried my BA twice and failed again."

Board members from the Mennonite Brethren Headquarters visited the Mahbubnagar mission station in 1958 with the intention of changing some policies.

The Board was particularly critical of older missionaries, those of us who had been in India for some time, saying that we were no longer needed in the field. "The Indian brethren are too dependent on you and you have become too involved," were some of their comments.

Yet indigenization was apparent in every phase of our work. Local preachers were responsible for building new churches, and membership was growing. They had obtained plots of land and oxen to farm or started small shops to supplement their meager salaries. Village mission schools administered by preachers and taught by teachers trained in the Mahbubnagar mission school were well attended.

The printing press in Mahbubnagar, with B. Aseervadam as manager, was printing the monthly periodical, songbooks, articles and pamphlets. Prayer halls were erected and supervised by lay preachers. Tract distribution was undertaken by laymen under the preacher's supervision.

The Mennonite Brethren High School in Mahbubnagar had reached peak enrollment. Potential students had to be turned away. Mr. D.J. Arthur, principal, and other qualified teachers were doing a commendable job.

Funding for various projects came less and less frequently from foreign donors. Tithing in many churches helped to pay preachers, Bible women and orphans. Some donations from the women's tithes also helped defray expenses at the printing press, for Bible school, for medicines, poor students and clothing for destitute widows.

Despite achievements and motivation to stay on, John and I, along with other older missionaries, were asked to complete our terms and not return to the Indian field.

If we had been allowed to continue the work until retirement, it would perhaps not have been necessary for the Board of Missions at a meeting in Hillsboro, Kansas, years later, to reflect that it had been a mistake to recall all the older missionaries.

After preparing bundles, consisting of a sheet, towel and some clothing, I labeled each with a number. Then I had each preacher, teacher or friend draw a number and match it with the number on the bundle. This way no favoritism was shown and each person got a gift. Packing and sorting took much of our time the last month we were in Mahbubnagar. John organized his accounts with D.J. Arthur who was principal of the school and ordered supplies for the coming year as we would not be returning. John hired laborers to continue the repairs of the buildings. This needed to be completed before the monsoon rains.

Driving to Chintakunta, Bethlehem, Kurmurti and other surrounding villages, we enjoyed the hospitality and curry and rice feeds of village friends and co-workers who wished to bid us farewell.

Leaving John with our luggage and a crowd of people, I took one last look at the bungalow and checked through the rooms, now swept bare, for anything we might have forgotten. Farewells were tearful as we said goodbye to dear friends and what had been our home for eighteen years. Many gave us flowers and garlands which hung heavy around our necks as we waved from the door of the train. Shouting *poi vastamu* (we'll go and come) in answer to those running beside the train saying *poi randi* (go and come), we watched the cluster of people until we rounded a corner and they were out of sight. John stood at the open door well after we had shunted over many tracks and were headed north past rocky hills and scrub.

Boarding the *S.S. Asia* in Bombay, we watched the Gateway of India and the city recede as the ship glided through the water. We did not know whether we would ever see the shores of Mother India again. We were sure, however, that "God meant everything for good" and that He would open other doors.

We spent much of our time on the deck of the ship as we sailed adjacent to the shores of Africa. The ship's Italian crew was courteous and every meal was a banquet.

After sailing through the Suez Canal, we enjoyed beautiful weather before mooring alongside the dock of Napoli. Bidding goodbye to our ship friends, we spent two weeks traveling through Italy, Switzerland and Germany before boarding the *S.S. Queen Elizabeth*. The portholes of the ship's cabin were just above water level and we watched the sea swell and spray. Not many passengers joined us on the ship's deck. It was getting cold and the windswept ocean rose and fell.

Our daughter Esther and other relatives met us at the busy pier in New York. After customs and the various procedures of re-entering America, we drove with Esther to Connecticut. Here we spent a few days with my sister, Lydia, and her husband, Dr. Charles Marple before proceeding to Kansas.

With the proceeds from forty acres of land in the Carson Township, Minnesota, which Father and Mother Wiebe had given us and which brother Jake had farmed for us in our absence, we bought a small house in Hillsboro, Kansas. John taught Missions, Bible subjects and acted as temporary Dean of Students at Tabor College while David and Paul attended classes. As Ebenfeld Church was without a pastor, John agreed to be their interim pastor for one year which was one of our best furlough experiences.

Living at home, Esther commuted to Goessel Hospital, where she was Nursing Superintendent. Next door to us in our newly acquired home, Irene and Donovan Janzen lived with their family, now numbering three sons.

John and Carol Wiebe with their three children resided in California while serving in the Children's Unit of Camarillo State Hospital. Herbert and V. Ruth had just returned with two sons from Indonesia where they had been with the Mennonite Central Committee.

The twins, Esther, Marilyn, John and I traveled south to Mexico during Christmas of 1959. The drive through arid rocky land and over scenic mountain passes — friendly, colorful people waved to us — reminded us of scenes in India.

After leaving Mexico City, a lively bustling metropolis, we visited some old Mennonite Settlements located on our route back to the United States. We ate corn and chicken enchilladas on New Year's Eve as we watched joyful Mexican children breaking *pinyatas* (decorated clay pots) each scrambling to retrieve the most sweets. After our three weeks vacation in Mexico, we returned to the cold in Kansas.

Still very interested in returning to India, John and I corresponded with Dr. M. Blanchard, the president of Ramapatnam Seminary on the sea coast of Andhra Pradesh. The Baptist group wrote to the Mennonite Brethren Board requesting them to lend us to teach in the Baptist Seminary and supervise the dispensary work in the hospital. This was an answer to our prayers and we joyfully accepted the offer.

Our twins, David and Paul, graduated the spring of 1960, cum laude, from Tabor College and were entered in "Who's Who" of Colleges. Enrolling our youngest in college, we began packing and preparing ourselves to return to India. We were delighted as well to attend at least two of our children's marriages. En route to David and Lorma's (Kroeker) wedding in Reedley, California, we visited John and Carol Wiebe. Then with the bridegroom, Paul, we drove to Fairview, Oklahoma, where he and Donna Beth (Kliewer) were married. John preached at both weddings. It was the last time our entire family was together.

A justly proud father with his sons

Book 4

1961-1970

The 707 plane we were traveling in arrived in Madras during the August heat. The forty-seven hour plane trip from New York took us via London, Prague, Geneva, Beirut and Bombay. John and I were tired but elated to return to India.

Still 153 miles south from where we would work, we boarded a mail train with our three suitcases for Tettu. There we were met by Dr. M. Blanchard who took us to their cool bungalow for a meal before being welcomed with garlands into the seminary fold.

Rev. Peter Jones and wife Babu, recent graduates of R.B.T. Seminary, whom John and I visited in their church in Bangalore.

Ramapatnam Seminary building. The Chapel, seating about 400, is upstairs, and four large classrooms with verandahs are downstairs.

The bungalow that was to become our home was built by a sea captain in the early 1900s. White ants had eaten into the heavy wood that supported the ceiling and these beams needed to be replaced. The foundations had also sunk and when it rained heavily, the floors on the east side of the bungalow sometimes were ankle-deep in water. John used chipped rock and cement to raise the floors and door frames one foot.

Our living quarters were upstairs. The dispensary cum hospital and patients' rooms comprised the downstairs of the bungalow.

Following the recent rains, the 111 acre Ramapatnam campus was verdant and beautiful. Butterflies by the hundreds fluttered around bright yellow and orange marigolds; others found nectar in the coral and red lilies that lined the paths. The Ghul Mohar was splendid with brilliant red flowers on trees with lacy green frond-like leaves. The Myna call and the screech of green-colored parakeets almost drowned out the "caw" of large black crows. Coconuts and Palmiras vied with the verdure of the Banyan, Neem and Tamarind trees. The trees offered mottled shade making the pre-monsoon heat bearable for the little half-clad children darting about collecting Neem berries. These berries were ground up for oil to use in tiny saucers. Wicks were placed in the oil to lighten up the darkness. The oil was also used for an ointment and sold for making soap.

Little boys and girls barely old enough to wield a stick herded their cattle and goats to patches of vegetation, sometimes breaking down a high branch for the hungry animals to be able to reach the leaves.

Such were a few of the *Sepia Prints* indelibly etched on our minds the first few days in Ramapatnam.

John and I thoroughly enjoyed the involvement in our new ministry, teaching eager, intelligent men and women. John taught Reformation, Church History and Letters to the Corinthians to advanced students working for their Bachelor of Divinity degrees in English.

I taught Old and New Testament Survey, Christian Doctrine, and Sunday school methods, in Telugu, and took charge of the seminary dispensary and rural clinics.

Ninety-seven students (many accompanied by their children), twelve teachers and their families, cleaners, gardeners, drivers, and hospital staff made up the seminary compound family.

For relaxation, John and I walked past the Christian cemetery, through mango groves, over stretches of sand, past millet fields to the Buckingham Canal. This canal was built from Madras to Guntur for transporting goods between cities during the late 19th century by hundreds of laborers who received grain for labor.

A weathered old man awaited us in his leaky boat to take us across the canal to the first village on the other side. Here, near the ocean, the Causarina trees, planted in rows, sheltered part of the sandy beach. Fisher folk, mending their nets and boats near the water, greeted us as we walked by.

Ramapatnam

Dr. and Mrs. M. Blanchard, president – center back row, and other faculty members with twenty-seven graduate students outside one of the four classrooms of the Ramapatnam Seminary

Vibrant, bandy legged, high spirited Florence had been in Ramapatnam since the early 1920s. Always dressed in an immaculate blue or white sari or dress with matching glass *gazulu* (bracelets), she was a well loved and respected missionary woman.

Early every morning, a cloud of dust followed Florence's four-wheel drive jeep, Deborah, as she affectionately called it, on her daily rounds visiting Bible women in the surrounding villages. One evening, honking and shouting, Florence drove up in time to hustle an obese merchant woman into the hospital just in time to deliver twins. The jolting and bumping over rutted roads had hastened the delivery.

The days Florence didn't drive to the villages, she taught for an hour or two in the seminary and took her turn in the chapel sessions in her inimitable way of expressing the truth.

Florence ate most of her meals with John and me. Always talkative, she questioned us about our morning activities while we enjoyed spicy shrimp, curry and rice. After telling us about the flat tire she had that morning and of Subbamma, the caste woman who was very interested in the Bible message, she said, "Viola, how many worm patients did you have today? How long was the tapeworm you removed from that little fellow?"

Suddenly John, who disliked discussions of such subjects at the dinner table, said, "Let's each say our favorite Bible verse before we dismiss for our further activities." I said mine, "I am with you always." John followed with "Casting all your care upon Him —" It was Florence's turn. "I rather like the one which says 'Fear not, thou WORM Jacob.'" At this, the three of us laughed heartily and John left the table.

After each of us had received a gift at Christmas dinner, Florence said, "Bula Dell, since you are the hostess, I put an extra gift for you under the tree."

"Oh, you shouldn't have," was our hostess' reply, but she untied the neatly wrapped parcel. A dozen tiny black frogs leaped out on Bula Dell who screamed and scattered the creatures. With a great deal of laughter, the rest of us retrieved the frogs and put them out into the night.

Several weeks later, Florence awakened one night to see a masked man leaning over her with a knife at her throat. "Get up, no sound, get me your money," he whispered, hurting her as he held her around the waist with one arm and with the other held the knife to her throat while pushing her to the back room. Florence recognized the voice to be that of the *Gurka* (guard) who had guarded a section of the compound and whom she had dismissed earlier for bothering the nurses.

Monthly payments for Bible women and school teachers were due at the end of each month and the *Gurka*, a refugee from Nepal, was aware that the money was with Florence.

"Let me put on a light so I can see," Florence declared.

He hissed, "Do not, or I will kill you," pulling her arm tighter.

She opened a cupboard where the paper money was hidden under towels, and managed to push the wads of money further back with her left arm while she found her small purse containing some money with her right hand. She handed the purse to her abductor. "Is that all?" he growled and shoved her roughly against the wall.

Not knowing whether he had gone, Florence stood until dawn singing to herself and repeating Bible verses. As fingers of light began to trace patterns across the floor and birds called, Florence ran to our bungalow and shouted, "Viola, John, come!"

We ran downstairs and reached her house just as she walked back and found where the miscreant had cut the screen on her verandah to enter her locked house. John reported the incident in Gudlur at the police station. Later the *Gurka* was found, still in possession of the purse minus the money. Florence had the cut screen mended and continued living in her little house for another six years.

Gathered under the shade of the Banyan and Ghul Mohar trees, villagers sat patiently, waiting to be seen at the clinic. Sitting with them were G. Maria or B. Rose or other faithful Bible women from nearby Tettu village. They sang and talked of the Great Physician who could heal both body and soul.

These servants of God came to the clinic once a week, sometimes bringing patients. They heard the complaints and commiserated with many villagers. "*Aunu* (yes)," the villagers said, "We know you. You were in our *palem* (section of a village) in summer after school closed and taught our children songs and stories which they then taught us. That was good. Will you come again next hot season?"

The Bible women walked many miles or rode on oxcarts to visit surrounding villages where they organized women's meetings and advised women regarding their rights and legal status. They often led church services when the preacher was absent or helped distribute milk powder and wheat to the most needy. For many nights and meals the Bible women were asked to stay in village homes, but they still carried a blanket and a tiffin carrier filled with food for the nights they spent on the verandah of a temple or home.

Rev. J. John and his wife Lillamma, a spiritually inspired couple, who served both church and villages with the Gospel of love in Jadcherla and other areas.

Far back – Missionary Irene Saunders in charge of Women's Work in the Ramapatnam area has become an Indian citizen and member of a village *panchayat* (committee). She has not left India since arriving in the 1920s.

The tallest, center right, is G. Maria, and B. Rose, far right, with other Bible women at a retreat in Tettu.

Blaise Lavai, in his book *Ask an Indian about India,* quoted Dr. S. Chandra Sekhar, then Minister of Health: "Roughly a third of all sickness and death is probably caused directly or indirectly by our extremely poor and depressing sanitation and public hygiene . . . If good drinking water is made available in every community . . . another third of the total sickness will disappear."

A normal once-a-week Ramapatnam clinic day began with a disheveled, hungry, poor group of patients who arrived early in the morning.

The visiting doctor, either Dr. Eaton or Dr. Mundhenk from the Ongole Hospital, arrived in a hospital van with a retinue of nurses, technicians and extra medicine.

Patients, some with tuberculosis and leprosy, many with itching bodies, running eyes, sores, scabies, many with worms, were registered by a nurse who gave them a ticket after they paid one rupee, the equivalent of ten cents. Then one by one, histories were recorded and the patients examined. Shown into another room, the patient was prescribed medication with some explanation and given the inevitable injection. Sometimes the nurses gave a shot of vitamins, calcium or even a placebo as the patient was not happy to leave unless he or she was given one.

We worked quickly in order to examine 200 or more patients between eight o'clock in the morning and six in the evening. Many were impatient to leave before dark so they could walk the long distances back to their villages or get a bus or *jatka* (horse carriage). A number of minor surgeries and sterilizations were performed after the crowd had been tended to. Some people were kept overnight in the hospital.

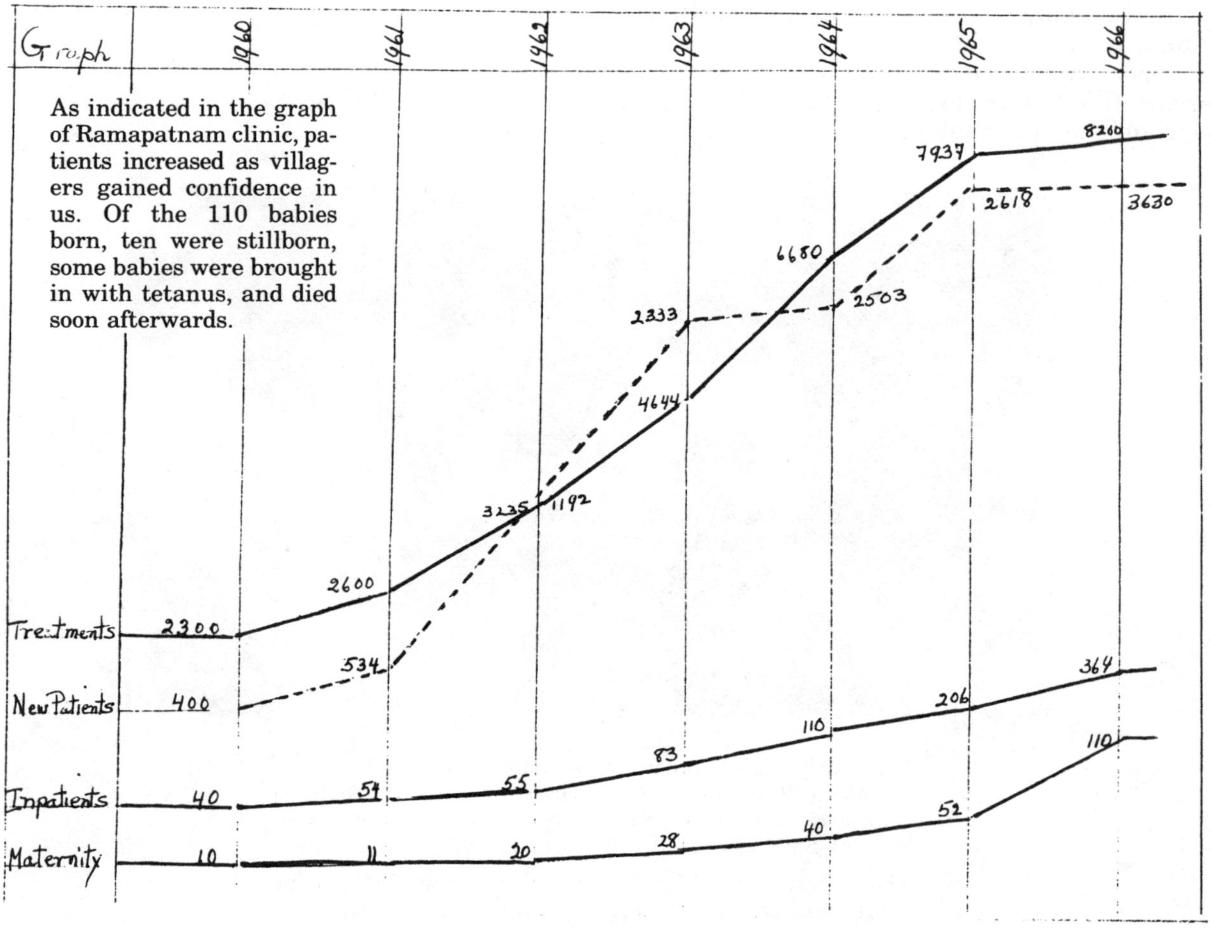

Graph

As indicated in the graph of Ramapatnam clinic, patients increased as villagers gained confidence in us. Of the 110 babies born, ten were stillborn, some babies were brought in with tetanus, and died soon afterwards.

	1960	1961	1962	1963	1964	1965	1966
Treatments	2300	2600	3235	4644	6680	7937	8260
New Patients	400	534	1192	2333	2503	2618	3630
Inpatients	40	54	55	83	110	206	364
Maternity	10	11	20	28	40	52	110

By western standards, our dispensary/hospital conditions were unhygienic and often disorderly. Perhaps the dispensary looked unkempt but the patients were much happier with their relatives near them. Children were allowed to accompany their mothers and every patient was allowed at least one *tordu* (helper). Often a patient could be seen nursing her child while sitting on the floor amid various cooking utensils and supplies from the market.

Hindus had their food cooked by their relatives in sheds we provided for this purpose.

We provided iron beds, thin coir mattresses, sheets, pillows and a light blanket. Linens were washed and ironed by the *dhobi* (laundryman) twice a week. Ankamma swept and washed all the floors and kept the squat latrines clean.

Certain days were not "auspicious" for patients to be discharged. Most did not want to leave the dispensary on even days but rather on the third, fifth or seventh day of the month.

Strict Muslim patients would not take a mouthful of water with their pills or medication before sundown during their *Ramadan* (fasting) period. During *Ramadan*, they also objected to their ears being syringed before sundown.

Because dentists were few and far between we frequently pulled teeth and put in temporary fillings. After the hollow of the tooth was cleaned with hydrogen peroxide, we mixed a small piece of cotton with oil-of-cloves and zinc oxide and placed this into the cavity of the tooth.

When we gave patients white aspirin for something other than headaches, they complained with "I don't have head pain." Realizing this, the Bangarapet Mission Pill Industry made aspirin in green, pink, and white so that this efficacious pill could be used for more than one purpose.

Krupadanam, one of our male nurses who was later dismissed for stealing medicine and charging patients more than the receipt showed, was reticent about helping with tetanus cases, convinced that the patients were contagious.

An elderly man who had been working with his horses in Tettu, was brought to us with a large infected cut. His relatives told us that he should be healed in our dispensary or not at all.

It was difficult to keep the man in a quiet dark room alone. Water from heavy rains was ankle-deep in the dispensary and had to be swept out periodically. People came and went and we had problems with space but we did the best we could. Unable to get his clenched jaws apart to give him liquid and food, I extracted two lower teeth and inserted a tube into his throat. We fed him this way and he slowly improved. Nagiah never forgot the care he received in the dispensary and brought many gifts of fruit, fish and vegetables in gratitude.

Some of the more common beliefs and superstitions of our patients were:

— That no water should be given to feverish patients and certainly not to those with diarrhea because "Won't more water make more stools?"

— That the yellow root, tumeric, was a good disinfectant and if taken regularly, would cure skin diseases.

— That "evil spirits could attack us if you wear white in the hospital ward. White is what widows wear."

— That the sacred tulasi *plant purified the blood.*

— That citrus fruit should not be eaten during the cool season for fear of getting colds or coughs.

— That babies should be given castor oil at birth and daily thereafter to ensure bowel elimination and to cleanse the body.

— That pregnant and postpartum women were only to eat white rice and chili powder in order to produce more milk.

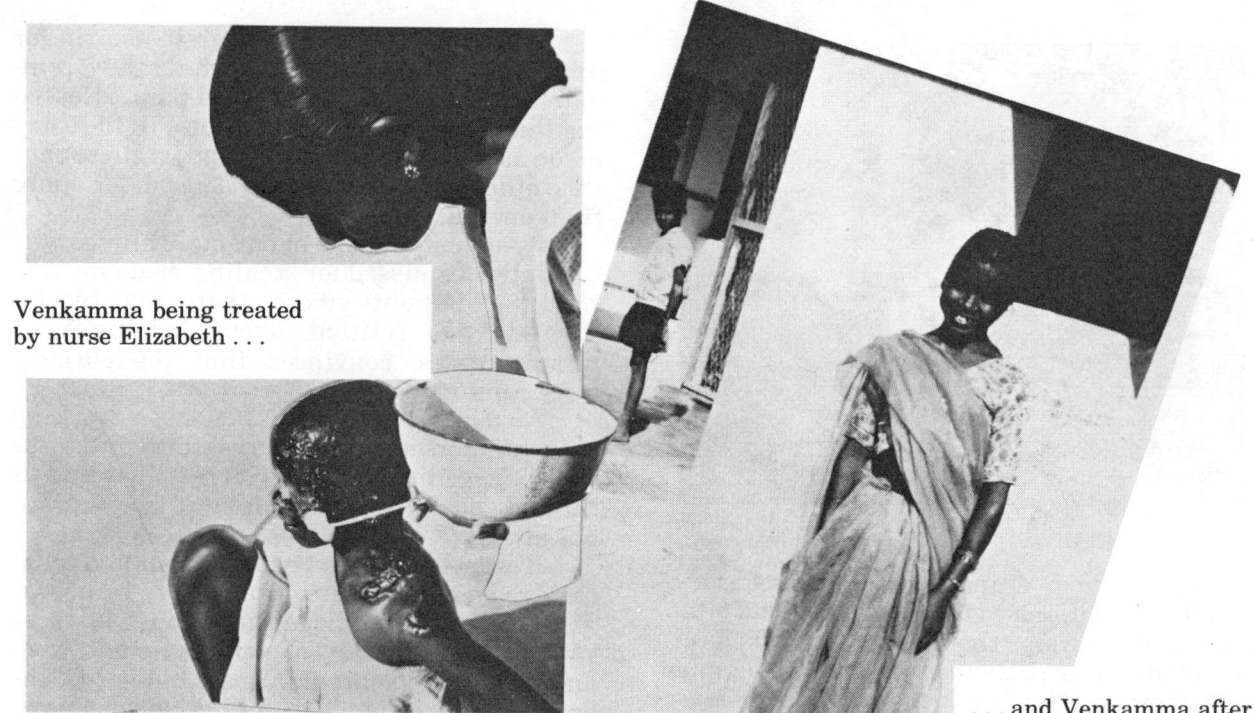

Venkamma being treated by nurse Elizabeth...

...and Venkamma after.

Venkamma was married at the age of twelve years. From the day she arrived at her husband's home, she had problems with her mother-in-law who scolded her relentlessly, convincing Venkamma she was useless. In loneliness and desperation, Venkamma poured kerosene over herself and lit a match. Villagers beat out the flames and with Venkamma's mother-in-law, brought her with second and third degree burns to the dispensary on a cart. Police cases, such as this one, were supposed to be taken to the government hospital, but they left Venkamma with us quickly and went. The villagers who brought her to us had no money and seldom visited the poor girl.

We often despaired about Venkamma. Her wounds started to heal and then began bleeding again. Both outer ears were burned off and only a portion of her mouth opened to allow the nurse or me to feed her liquid foods. We applied Gentian Violet to her burns as much as necessary and she slept without clothes under a mosquito net.

Venkamma never again became a pretty sight but eventually she did heal. Her smile was radiant and she felt peace when she accepted Christ as her Savior. After she became ambulatory, she did odd jobs around the hospital, until we sent her to her own parents' home.

During *Diwali* (Festival of Lights), a number of burn cases appeared at the dispensary. Villagers placed oil lamps around their huts and along walls and steps. One little six-year old girl's skirt caught on fire and she was taken to the government hospital with eighty percent of her body burned. Her burns became infected and she died. Soon after this, another burned child from the same village was brought to our dispensary. She survived and our reputation for healing patients spread far and wide.

A frail old woman walking home at day's end, carrying a bundle of sticks, suddenly stumbled. The sticks fell on the path and she on top of them. How long she lay there bleeding from a deep gash on her cheek, she couldn't say. A passerby found her and brought her to the dispensary. Esther, our daughter, was home for a visit and was courageous enough to sew up the gash with a surgical needle too large for facial sutures, but it was the only one we had.

After a day or two, the old woman went home with her cheek bandaged. Several months later, she returned to greet and show us her wound which was completely healed. Only a long raised scar showed where the gash had been.

"Let us fully live the Life Thou hast given us. Let us bravely take and bravely give. This is our prayer to Thee." Rabindranath Tagore

At four o'clock in the morning when the stars paled in the sky and the air was still cool, villagers began to walk towards the clinic.

Some of the men, naked except for a *dhoti* (loin cloth) wrapped around the waist and a *ramalu* (turban), walked ahead of their wives and daughters, anxious to be the first in the line of villagers waiting to be attended to at the clinic. For hours they squatted on the verandah or lay down on a cloth spread under the Banyan trees, always patient.

I began taking histories and examining the patients. A man sat opposite me. "What is your trouble, Pitchiah?"

"When I lie down, it says 'dar da-dar da' here," he said pointing to his chest.

Another said, indicating his abdomen, "So many times there is a 'gurra-gurra' sound here," (rolling his Rs). A woman with a drawn face, squinted at us through watery eyes and insisted her head said 'dub-dub,' like the sound of breaking stones. Yet another told us her history of having 'kee-ee' noises like a cricket in her ears.

Having been given the necessary medicines and injections, for they were not happy leaving without something, some patients walked away only to return after reaching the gate. "Was I to take the pills with hot or cold water?" "Were the pills to be taken before or after I eat?"

After reassuring them again and encouraging them to eat nutritious foods to stay well, they went on their way saying, *"Poi vastaamu* (we will go and come again)."

One tall, gaunt man named Baliah, who had been ill a long time, was given a large bottle of mixture, much diluted so he would not swallow toxic amounts, came back two days later with an empty bottle. "Why are you back already, Baliah? We gave you enough medicine for a week." "Amma, if this medicine can make me better in a week, surely it will help me in two days."

An old man, bent at the shoulders from age and burdens, handed me a large cock that had been in a *pandemu* (cockfight) and had a large gash down its breast. He held the squawking bird as I stitched it and proudly told me that his cock had won the last fight

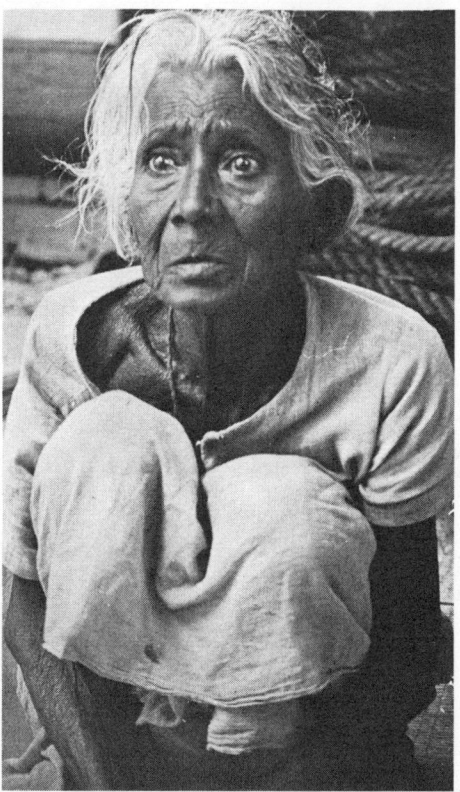

All Adamma needed was shelter and nourishing food.

and earned him five rupees. I suggested he not use the cock again and watched the old man hobble away with his colorful cock tucked under his arm. A number of villagers brought me their animals to heal. I did what I could if the ailment was obvious.

Quite frequently, while making rounds in the clinic in the evening, I found the patient on a mat on the floor and her *tordu* (helper) and children crowded on the bed. Leaving the night nurse with final instructions, I wound my way among the patients and their companions to check on Adamma whom we had found on the side of the road. She was lying on a mat on the verandah wrapped in a thin sheet, sleeping quietly.

```
Statement of the Village Munsif, Ramapatnam
Kandukur Taluk, Nellore District. January 28, 1964.

Rev. John A. Wibbe died of asphixiation from drowning
on the sea shore of the Bay of Bengal near Inspection Bungalow
at Ramapatnam on 28th December 1963.

                                        Village Munsif
                                        Ramapatnam.
```

John carefully eased a gold bracelet onto my arm together with a kiss. It was Christmas 1963. "Don't only widows wear metal bracelets?" John said. I laughed, thanking him and said, "Wives also are delighted to wear them."

No one sensed anything but the brilliance of the afternoon on the warm beach on 28 December 1963. Esther interrupted her language studies for mission work to visit us in Ramapatnam for the Christmas season.

We walked with friends to the canal, boarded the small boat pulled by men to the coolness of a waving causarina grove where we were to picnic. Most of those present could not swim but waded and enjoyed the water.

After he had given Esther a few lessons in swimming, John said, "I want to swim out further." He then raised both his arms to us, smiled and swam out to sea. That was the last time I saw my John alive. The undertow took him under and no one present could swim enough to venture out in the strong current. Finally fishermen passed and we persuaded them to assist John. Holding onto one another's arms and a large piece of wood, they brought John's seemingly lifeless form back to those of us hopefully, fearfully waiting. Esther and I immediately tried to resuscitate him. Others helped with massaging John and with reassuring words.

Dr. Blanchard drove to Kavali and back to bring a doctor, oxygen and injections, but by 8:00 p.m. we were all forced to accept that John had crossed to another shore.

John's body was tenderly washed and dressed by Esther and me. Hundreds of fisherfolk, students, caste and outcaste, educated and illiterate, Christian, Muslim and Hindu came to mourn with me. They all wept bitterly and pronounced his death not only a severe blow to the seminary but to each of us personally.

A Telugu service was held in the seminary chapel and then "My Beloved" was laid to rest in a simple coffin lined with a white sheet and black cloth in the mission graveyard in Ramapatnam.

MISSIONARIES

April 29, 1964

Our Dear Friends: Readers of the Challenger:

Verse two of Psalm 18 is a striking one, and I'd like you to turn with me to this wonderful consolation—"my rock, my fortress, my deliverer, my God, my strength, my buckler, my salvation, my high tower." So why should my soul be charged with care—"His eye is on the sparrow, and I know He watches me."

With the help of the Lord, I am trying to adjust to a new way of life, but there are many moments of loneliness. Your letters full of loving sympathy have done much for me, and I thank you.

"Death is but the graduation from training in this world to the real life in eternity," and John is with Him, whom he loved and served.

Four months have passed since the Lord took my beloved companion to His reward. He has given an inner calm, which has not been untroubled by conflicts and longings, but nonetheless peace, which passes understanding.

The Lord's provision in sending Esther is of course a constant comfort. She keeps everyone happy with her enthusiasm, new ideas, and trusting calm. Young and old appreciate her and the Lord has much work for her, for which He has prepared her well. To work in this country (or any land) now, (or any time) takes courage and stamina and faith. Praise God, all are to be had for the asking.

For the duration of the hot season, we will be in Kodaikanal. Esther has four or five hours with the munshi, language teacher, and I will continue to answer the many (500 or more) letters which have come to us, and keep coming. Many of you will have received "John—the Beloved Missionary" tribute letter, and we hope you will consider this a reply to your kind letters.

The unhealed wound is often touched again as vegetable vendors, shoe makers, hawkers, coolies alike, come to weep and offer their condolences and say how much John's kind words meant to them. "Little deeds of kindness" in the name of the Lord, bring their reward.

"May the left arm be under your head and the right arm of the Lord surround you."

With congratulations to the new editor, and thanks for the Challenger, and greetings of love in our Lord, to each of you.

                                              Viola C. Wiebe
                                              (Mrs. John A.)

Kodaikanal, India.
June 1964.

Dear Friends,

How comforting to be with Esther, and read letters from my other children as we sit on the porch of our rented stone cottage in the cool sunny beauty of Kodai, away from the heat of the plains for a short time. The wonder of God's beauty who can fathom? The hills are ablaze with rhododendron. On the mossy crags, up steep inclines and on limbs of trees, climb porcelain-like orchids of many varieties. May was the month of larkspur, osbeccia, foxglove, antignon, petunias, dhalias, gladiola. What is there left for July? Myriads of fragile yellow mimosa burst forth, scenting the hillsides intermingling with the smoke of eucalyptus fires.

The sun has set. It is chilly enough to go indoors and throw some pine-cones on the fire, as we wait for our friends Drs Jack and Naomi Curman from Vellore, to join us for supper around the fireplace.

           Blessings on you—
                  Viola.

...1967

"These past years have been a kaleidoscope of activities. To put all these changing scenes into one letter poses quite a problem.

"Having been granted a six-month furlough or 'change of occupation,' I left with Ruth Thurmond and Alice Findlay in early May for an unforgettable journey through the Holy Land and adjacent countries. We were out of Tel Aviv two days before war in Israel was declared. We continued our trip on to Greece and Rome."

"Ready to Go Back," Says 40-Year Missionary to Southern India

Mrs. Viola (John A.) Wiebe of the Delft (Minnesota) Mennonite Brethren Church was scheduled to arrive in India November 15 after a short furlough in the United States.

I visited three of my children who reside in the United States and stayed with brothers and sisters scattered around the country. As I spoke in many churches and centers, I experienced a zeal for missions, with generous contributions towards mission work.

The six months were over quickly and I returned to Ramapatnam. Although John was no longer with me it was good to return to the seminary. I taught seventeen second-year students in a class of "Life of Christ" and thirty-five first-year men and women "Sanitation, Disease and First Aid." The rest of my time was taken up with the dispensary, traveling to villages, women's conventions, center meetings and church gatherings.

"It is dusk, the colors of the monsoon sky are fading into quieter shades. Soon the sun dips and twilight lies warm on the sand.

"Women hurry home from their field work. Some have been cutting grass, others gathering sticks which are tied together in bundles and balanced on their heads. Still others have been cutting grain and carrying baskets of millet. Small children who have played all day near their mothers walk alongside thinking of the *chapatis* (flat unleavened bread) they will soon dip into savory curry and eat before they fall asleep on the piece of mat or sack spread on the dirt floor of the village hut.

"There is a deep rumble of thunder. The black heavens empty their contents in sheets. Frogs increase their crescendo and the humid air wraps around us. Darkness is thick but the light of the gospel shines in many hearts.

"Returning from the program in the village, our car sinks into the mud hub-deep. Two teams of buffalo and several men work hard to pull us out.

"Softly waving Neem trees, stately palms, rustling mango trees all bespeak the greatness of our Maker. The heavy scent of jasmine and other flowering shrubs with heavy blossoms, intermingle with the odor of pungent cooking. We are nearing a home of caste

"Buffalo, cows, goats and sheep plod homeward, urged on by small shepherd boys. Later the men will bring the farm implements and the oxen home to food and rest.

"The white-winged paddy bird, which has been feeding in the shallow pond, rises to join other birds already roosting in the trees. Crows and flying fox noisily find their roosts while huge bats start their forage for bugs and fruit.

"Fourteen five to nine-year olds are giving a program in church together with songs, scriptures and stories all in beautiful unison. Nearly an hour without a break.

"Suddenly, as if a curtain has come over us, it is night. Stars twinkle as the orchestra of an Indian night begins. Mosquitoes hum, frogs croak, crickets chirp, dogs bark, drums, flutes and talking blend together.

people. Those not engaged in cooking, come to the front court and bid us be seated. A frail, lustrous eyed woman tells us, 'I have had ten children, nine have died in infancy. Only one son is living . . .'

"Our meal finished, we thank our kind hosts and take our leave. The rain has ceased. From the window of the car I can see myriads of shining stars: The Heavens declare the Glory to God . . . the firmament showeth His handiwork."

Viola Wiebe.

Written for the "Zionsbote," a Mennonite Brethren journal.

Before leaving for the hills in 1964, Esther, who was studying for her Telugu exam in Nellore, found some professional snake charmers and brought them with their baskets, *Eesera bark* and *gourd fifes* (flutes) to the campus in Ramapatnam.

Snakes had been seen frequently at the seminary. Florence Rowland, a fellow missionary, held a small cobra against her bedroom wall with a stick shouting, "*Neynu pattukoleynu* (I can't hold it any longer)," until help came to kill the snake.

The snake charmers whose hands were scarred and with some fingers missing (cut off after being bitten), began to play their fifes near a large Banyan tree. They sat cross-legged, swaying slowly, while playing when two large cobras slithered from the tree. The snakes were caught by two of the men while the third man caught five kraits from another branch of the tree where the roots hung to the ground.

The snake charmers put the reptiles sedated with the *Eesera bark* into their covered baskets. Amazed, we accompanied the men to another magnificent large Banyan tree not fifteen yards from our kitchen door. From this tree, a seven-foot cobra, among other cobras, kraits and Russel's Vipers responded to the snake charmer's music. An ever-increasing number of spectators were awed by the largest, most beautifully marked Russel's Viper anyone had ever seen. It measured about a yard in length and two and a half inches in diameter. Tired after catching forty-three snakes, the men talked of leaving but we persuaded them to continue.

Three more kraits and six large cobras were caught in areas thought unlikely places by the crowd, but true to the charmers' intuition, snakes were found. The men were asked how they knew snakes would be present. They replied, "A certain scent comes to our nostrils."

That night, the three men with their catch of fifty-three snakes sedated in their baskets, slept on our verandah. Early the next morning, they had already been to a neighboring *palem* (small village) to drink *toddy* (local brew) and were quite intoxicated.

Two very large cobras had been sighted in the vicinity of the graveyard and the men were guided towards John's grave. There, the largest cobra yet was coaxed out and taken captive.

By this time, the admired snake men were becoming careless. One of them suddenly winced and removed his finger from the snake's mouth with some effort. He held his finger tightly and turned the cobra over to his companion. We asked the man a number of times whether he had been bitten. The man held out his finger in response. Esther ran to the dispensary which was nearby for anti-venom and a syringe. By the time she returned, the man had a slow pulse, was stiffening and foaming from the mouth. His eyes rolled back. The man's companions were also alarmed and were grinding up assorted leaves and bark to pour down the man's throat. Meanwhile, Esther injected the anti-venom intravenously, then called for the others to load the jeep. She drove the three men, their equipment and fifty-four snakes to Nellore Hospital. There the bitten man received a repeat of the I.V. anti-venom. His companions refused to leave him at the hospital and took him to the village.

Since distances were great and communication difficult, Esther and I thought we would never find out what happened to the snake charmer.

A couple of mornings later, however, we met all three men at the railway station carrying their heavy baskets bound for the big city. The man who had been bitten put his hand in the open window of the car and said *Vandanamulu* (thank you) before boarding the train. In Madras, the snakes would be milked of their thick venom to make anti-venom serum and the skins of the snakes would be used for belts, purses and shoes for export.

During the month of November, after torrential rains, when cool breezes from the sea refreshed us, Solomon Raju, the mission dispensary ambulance driver, died.

I had gone to Ongole, forty miles northwest of Ramapatnam, to a women's convention at which I was to be one of the speakers. While sweeping the dining room after I left, Laxmi heard what she thought was an uncommon noise coming from the kerosene refrigerator. Worried, she called Solomon Raju who was talking to some patients at the dispensary to come and check.

I had always regulated the refrigerator myself and had filled the large tank with kerosene before leaving for Ongole. I knew I would be gone for several days. The driver, hearing a sputtering sound, jerked out the kerosene tank. Kerosene spilled and caught fire from the wick that was still burning. Solomon Raju, who was wearing a nylon shirt, was also splashed with kerosene and became a flaming torch. He shouted and ran through two rooms of the bungalow out to the verandah and threw himself into a puddle of water.

By this time, nurses and patients, hearing the commotion, rushed out and put out the flames. They carefully placed his charred body into the hospital van and drove him to the Nellore Hospital where Dr. M. Boehr and the nurses did all they could for him.

While I was giving a talk at the women's conference a runner brought me the message concerning Solomon Raju's accident. I read the message, then asked the women present to pray with me for Solomon Raju, closed my speech and took the next bus to Nellore. Seeing our energetic, willing night-or-day driver swathed in bandages lying rigidly in bed troubled me greatly. I took his unbandaged hand as I prayed.

He opened his eyes and haltingly said, "Amma . . . I am sorry about the refrigerator . . . When I get well . . ." "Solomon Raju," I said, my voice breaking, "All of us here and in Ramapatnam are praying for you and we only want you to get better."

He thanked me and closed his eyes saying, "I accepted Christ while working with you . . ."

Three days later, he was relieved of his suffering and went to meet his Maker. We sorrowed and so did his wife and five children, but "Not as those who have no hope, for we knew we would meet in Glory."

The government and mission gave no social security or compensations for the widow when her husband died. This matter concerned me and I wrote a number of letters to the mission and government officials regarding the matter, but received little response other than "we will look into the matter."

Our dispensary staff gave Sugunama, the widow, a lump sum and several months of Solomon Raju's salary to defray some of her expenses and help her children in school. She then moved back to her parents' home in Nellore where she lived with her children.

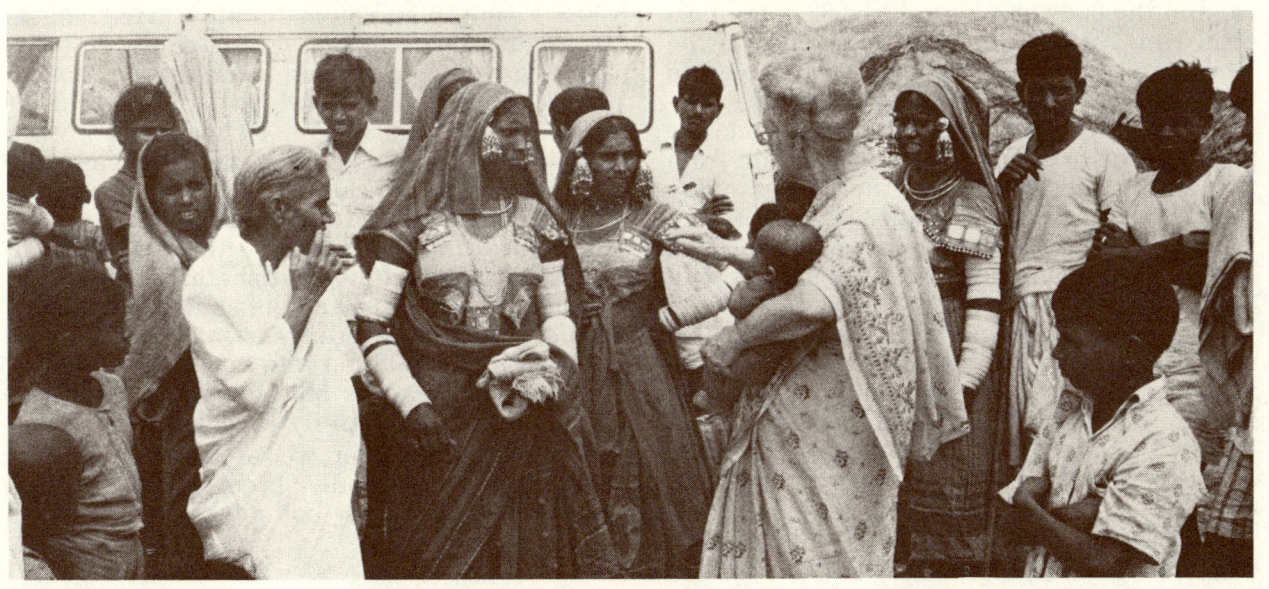

A yearly function which became a tradition, was *Baby Day*. Mothers who delivered their babies in our hospital, brought the children for a tea party, health lessons, gifts and devotions. It was encouraging to note that most had tried to follow our instructions, in feeding and caring for their babies, and in bringing them for their injections regularly.

The patient's history had been written down. Checking with the stethoscope, I found that the baby the patient was carrying had no heartbeat. It was obvious that the fetus was already dead and we decided to send the women immediately to the Ongole Hospital forty miles away.

The woman died after reaching the hospital and the body was brought back in the hospital van. I wanted to have her buried in the Christian cemetery but the husband pled to be allowed to take the body to his village eleven miles away. There, he tried to persuade the local barber to remove the unborn child from the womb after they gave the barber *toddy* (local brew) to drink. He refused. The husband then took his wife's body to the woods and tied it to a tree, leaving the remains for the wild dogs and animals.

I heard later that with this particular sub-caste if the woman died before the fetus was born, the unborn child had to be removed before the woman could be buried. Had I known this, we would have done a C-section at the dispensary with or without a doctor present.

Often women were brought to the dispensary after village midwives had done everything they could to deliver the child and had failed.

One woman gave birth to her fifth daughter. The baby was quietly sleeping next to the mother in a crib. I was in the adjoining room checking patients when Elizabeth, the nurse, rushed in exclaiming that the newborn child was hardly breathing.

I went in and immediately started mouth-to-mouth resuscitation on the child. The tiny baby gave a wheeze and from its right nostril came a bit of thread which I pulled and removed a wad of string. I checked the other nostril and found more wads of thread. The awful realization came to me that the mother had tried to suffocate her child.

Speaking gently to the mother, I tried to help her understand that she had a beautiful daughter. The husband, a fisherman from the *palem* (section of village) nearby, was called in and he too told his wife that their daughter would some day be able to do *coolie* (porter) work to help the family's income.

A few days later, we sent the woman with her child home. Sadly, I learned that after a few weeks, the baby had died.

A frail fisherman's wife who already had eight children, delivered twins, a boy and a girl. Her husband drank heavily and the mother begged me to take her daughter. She already had several daughters who would need to present *dowries* (property and money to their husbands) and favored her son who was lighter complexioned and would take care of her in her old age.

I typed a paper stating that the baby had been handed over to me and had the mother thumbprint it. The village headman also signed the paper and little Talitha came under my guardianship.

From that time on, there were others who brought their little ones or delivered them in the dispensary asking us to take the children. Our little adopted tribe grew. During the day, the nurses helped care for the babies and at night, we hired a widow, Ankamma, to take charge.

One young mother practically threw her little scrap of a girl away. The child had been fed on rice water since birth, the mother had no milk and the baby tipped the scales at four pounds. Tara Bai tripled her weight in six months with care and good nourishment and became a sturdy, curly haired child.

Yelliah, with tears in his eyes, brought me a little bunch of rags on which lay a two and a half pound premature baby so thin and dehydrated with welts all over her body from bites. "*Dayachesi*, Amma, take care of my daughter. Her mother died ten days ago." I took the baby and she soon began to thrive.

Little Joel had not been well since birth. One day only one month old, he began spitting up blood and died quietly in Elizabeth's arms.

Jothi, Timothy, James, Moses and Pankajam joined Talitha and Tara Bai. The dispensary staff and I checked prospective parents very carefully before finding permanent homes for the children. Nurse Elizabeth adopted Talitha, the first of our special children.

One Day

"Amma," Elizabeth the night nurse calls from downstairs, "a very sick woman has come." It can't already be 5:00 a.m. but checking the clock, I see it is just that.

Taking a quick shower and putting on clothes the *dhobi* (laundryman) has brought the day before, I hurry down to the dispensary, the bottom floor of the bungalow. Amul wags his tail as the door creaks open. Sugurnamma, who sleeps on the verandah adjoining mine, follows me down the stairs and locks the door after me.

Two women with *saris* pulled over their heads *salaam* (greet) me before they lead me to a woman miserable with fever. "We will do what we can and God will do the rest," I say, checking her heartbeat and lungs. Her temperature reads 103 and I suspect typhoid but we will observe her for a day or two. Putting her into a clean cot, we continue our rounds.

"Is Balamma ready to take her baby home?" I ask Elizabeth.

"Yes, but she is waiting for her relatives to bring a coconut so she can break it and spill the milk at the entrance of the dispensary."

"How is Papamma?" I ask as I pull the sheet back from a woman with a vacant stare lying quietly in bed. "*Bagunnava?* (Are you well?)" There is no response but we hope that it is just a matter of time before she speaks. Papamma's mother cooks for her and feeds her six-week old baby with a bottle.

"Elizabeth, you have been awake all night, go and rest, Helen will take over now." "All right, Amma, if you will go and have your breakfast." Affectionately, I watch the slight figure with the thick black hair coiled at the nape of her neck retreat.

"Helen, have you someone to care for your children today?"

"My Mother is with them," she answers, folding the pleats of her spotless white sari as she prepares to start her shift.

It is now 6:45 a.m. Time enough to shower, put on a clean sari and blouse, and have tea and toast before I must be at the seminary. Cook Daniel hovers near the table as I eat and asks, "Will there be guests for lunch today? If the Pallepalem village women bring *royalu* (shrimp), shall I make extra curry?"

"Miss Rowland will be back from Gudlur village and there may be others so perhaps boil extra drinking water and heat bath water, please."

"Amma," Daniel complains, "we can't get enough buffalo milk, even in Kavali. Perhaps if I hear of someone driving to Nellore, I will inform you so that we can order some food supplies?"

"*Manchidi* (good), Daniel."

Nurse O. Elizabeth holding Talitha's hand, S. Sugurnamma and I

One Day, cont.

Sugurnamma, who sweeps and cleans the bungalow, is a happy girl these days. I have helped arrange marriage for her with one of the seminary men. Requesting her to prepare the guest room for the visitors, I collect my books and papers.

It is a brilliant morning and Amul capers beside me as I walk to the seminary chapel. Villagers coming for vaccinations *salaam* (greet) me and I tell them that the nurse will take care of them at the dispensary. As I hurry on, small red berries from the Banyan trees drop on the dust near my feet as the monkeys chatter and climb about the branches.

Climbing up the steps of the hundred year old seminary made with hardened earth blocks, I hear singing accompanied by *tablas* (drums). Professors take turns several times a month to lead the chapel hour. Leaving my *chappulu* (sandals) near the door, I hurry in because they have started punctually as usual.

As soon as the chapel exercises are over, we disburse for classes. Twenty eager first and second-year students wait for me to teach Survey of the Old and New Testament. One of them is absent today as her baby is sick.

After class, I visit the students' quarters to check on Shanti's baby and other little ones under the care of two *ayahs* (nurses) while their mothers attend classes. Others, who are not attending seminary, invite me into their homes to have a cup of tea or to see the gardens they've started to grow. I encourage one or two of the women to burn the rubbish collecting near their houses.

Near midday, I walk back to the dispensary where Helen, the nurse, has taken the histories of a number of patients, has repeated medication for others and has admitted a few new patients to the dispensary. The ward has formerly been only for women and children until the men objected with "Don't we also get ill?" Asking the Board of Directors for extra funding, we extended the verandah for men patients. "Perhaps we will have some respite during the heat of the noon hour," I tell Helen while I watch her wipe the sweat from her face with the end of her sari.

The quiet interlude is short, however. A carload of visitors arrive soon after lunch. After showing the visitors where to wash the dust off their feet, I return to the dispensary. Helen is upset because one of the patients refuses to take her medicine and another has vomited in the admitting room.

"Amma, the ward *ayah* is not here yet to clean up," she complains.

Taking a bucket and some rags, I clean up the mess while Helen remarks with some embarrassment, "Amma, you, as a foreigner, have your status assured, but I would demean myself to be a cleaning woman. The patients would have no respect for me."

Just as we put the rags in the sun to dry, a woman heavy with child is admitted. On examining her, I realize she has two fetal heartbeats. Soon the woman is on the delivery table. Two healthy babies are born and we lead the mother to the ward where her two little ones are laid by her side.

Checking my watch, I find it is time to walk with my guests to the village. Helen reassures me that she can handle the dispensary until Elizabeth comes to take over.

On the way to Buckingham Canal, the guests and I pass a group of wailing villagers. A child now lying on the sand had fallen into the water hole and is in distress. I ask one of the guests to help me. We pick up the child, keeping his head down to expell as much water as possible, and carry him back to the dispensary. The worried grandmother and some other villagers run along beside us. When we reach the dispensary, we suction more water from the child's lungs, put him into a clean bed and watch him fall asleep before joining the other guests under the Causarina trees.

We relax as we watch the sun sink into the sea, and watch fishermen check their nets for fish. Finally we return to the bungalow for dinner. This evening there will be a welcome meeting given by the seminary student body for the guests.

The night breeze rustles the palms and coaxes sweet scent from the Queen-of-the-Night blossoms as we walk back home enjoying the sea air. Just as we round the corner close to the dispensary, someone runs towards us, "Amma . . ."

"The Church is planted, not yet a fully grown tree. Lift up your eyes and look to the fields for they are white to harvest," John 4:35-36.

"I believe the development in the process of church planting by the Mennonite Brethren Mission was the result of the guidance of the Holy Spirit and prayerful planning on the part of the missionaries.
— "Today there are 700 villages where all the pastors and preachers live in their own villages with their congregations and where the churches are called local churches and not affiliated churches of the mother mission compound church.
— "The entire brotherhood met for the first time as a convention in 1918 with a membership of 2100. It has since met annually and has become the organization through which the Telugu Mennonite Brethren Church finds its expression.
— "The next unifying step was when the missionary council and the native Field Association were combined into a joint field council.
— "The administrative positions have been transferred to the national brethren. The administrative committee of the Bible School, the educational institutions, are managed by nationals. The editor of the conference monthly periodical, the radio pastor, the scriptwriter of the broadcasting programs and the manager of the printing press are nationals.
— "The challenge confronting the church in India in 1971 with 530 million people, more than a seventh of the world's population, is that only 2.5 percent are Christians. There are two million people in the Mennonite Brethren mission field area and only ten percent of the Mennonite Brethren Christians are educated."

The above excerpts from an article written by D.J. Arthur in the "Suvartamani (Good News)," May 1971, on "Church Planting in the Mennonite Brethren Field of India."

"Die Sach ist Dein, oh Herr"
The work is Thine, oh Lord.

It should never cease to excite us that Christians are involved in a world-wide cause — John 3:16. The message of the love of God in Christ Jesus, which has brought so many to the Light was proclaimed by His ambassadors. This Good News will continue to be told from generation to generation.

Indian leaders have often come under Christian influence or have, at some time, attended a Christian institution. Dr. Radha Krishnan, former President of India, said, while traveling through Mahbubnagar, "Christians are an ordinary people with an extraordinary message."

In the *Illustrated Weekly of India*, 4 January 1970, Khushwant Singh, editor, had this to say:

"I praise foreign missionaries because they initiated and are even today the driving force behind most organized Christian endeavor.

— "Consider how many Hindus, Muslims and Sikhs were born in Christian maternity homes, educated in Christian schools and colleges, and treated in Christian hospitals.

— "Consider the sacrifices made by men and women who abandon the comforts and security of life in Europe and America to run these maternity homes, schools colleges and hospitals.

— "Consider what we owe these people who work among our poorest Harijans (outcastes), orphans, abandoned women and children, the blind and the handicapped.

— "And then consider the ingratitude of those who without any proof whatsoever accuse them of base motives, of bribery to win adherents or serving foreign political interests.

— "We give the generations of foreign missionaries who worked and gave their lives to serve India, our grateful thanks."

KHUSHWANT SINGH
M.P.

49-E, SUJAN SINGH PARK,
NEW DELHI - 110003.

Date 25 Aug '75

Dear Mrs Wiebe,

a million thanks and the Guru's blessings on all your journey. Of course take whatever you like of my article. I have often written articles on the excellence work done by Christian missions (I am a product of St. Stephens College — so is my wife) and the crass ingratitude of the Hindu chauvinists. Not to worry most Indians love & respect you as much as I.

Yrs Khushwant Singh

Farewell Address Presented To

MRS. VIOLA WIEBE

By

THE SEMINARY FAMILY, RAMAPATNAM

Dear Madam,

It is with immense sorrow that we the members of the Seminary family have assembled here this evening to bid you an affectionate farewell on the eve of your departure from our midst.

Our hearts are filled with deepest gratitude to God for your practical and unselfish christian life which has evoked our highest esteem and admiration for you. During your tenure of office as the Manager of the Dispensry, you have developed not only the building but also the number of the beds and the propogation of the Gospel to hundreds of people on all Thursdays. The members living on the Campus and those outside were thrilled to talk about your saintly character, your childlike simplicity and love for every one irrespective of caste or creed, poor or rich and great or small. Your Evangelistic zeal and fervour with unostentatious christian service are a rich heritage that you have bestowed on us to cherish and emulate in our daily lives.

The members of the Seminary family always wondered at your distribution of Food supplies and clothing to all the poor people in the surrounding places. It has become a slogan among the people of Mocherla Reddipalem, Salipet, Ramapatnam and Pallepalem that you are a " LOVELY CHRISTIAN MOTHER OF THE CAMPUS ". When the poor mothers were unable to support their children you have become a shelter to the children by taking them under your care.

Madam, the sacrifice you have made by holding on to the work in the Seminary inspite of the sudden demise of your beloved husband, our saintly guru a few years back, shall ever remain in our memories as an example of your love for service above anything else.

The special abilities you have manifested in Chapel talks with beautiful and meaningful illustrations are instructive and inspirational As you have been an active, energetic and sociable to all the people in the Seminary Campus, we assure you that we will a l w a y s r e m e m b e r and earnestly pray for heaven's richest blessings upon you.

Madam, kindly accept this small gift as a token of our appreciation and love for your noble service and convey our greetings to all your chiidren and their families. We bid you God's speed and we shall be looking forward to welcoming back to Ramapatnam in to our midst your dear daughter Miss Esther Wiebe, who has already won the affection of our hearts.

RAMAPATNAM,
25th March 1970

Yours in His service,
THE MEMBERS OF THE SEMINARY FAMILY.

1970

My final days of mission work in India were spent balancing and handing over accounts and responsibilities and completing projects.

Despite multiple interruptions, cupboards and boxes of accumulated things had to be sorted and much given away.

How shall I ever forget those final goodbyes. Tears flowed as those who had been close came to bid farewell — those whom we loved and who loved us in return. I was leaving the country where my dear John was buried and our best years had been spent; where our children had been born — the land of our adoption.

"In every nation God has those who worship Him, and do good deeds and are acceptable to Him — — you have heard about the Good News --- that there is peace with God through Jesus, the Messiah, who is Lord of all creation". Acts: 10: 35, 36 (L.B.)

"Much is required from those to whom much is given; for their responsibility is greater"
Lu: 12: 48.

AMERICAN MOTHERS COMMITTEE

of

Certificate of Merit

Presented to

Viola Catherine (Bergthold) Wiebe

Whose outstanding qualifications as an ideal Mother caused her to be singled out as a nominee for selection as State Mother of Kansas, 1961.

In recognition of this distinction she is hereby honored.

NATIONAL PRESIDENT   Margaret Selfridge, STATE CHAIRMAN

I·HAVE CHOSEN·YOU & ORDAINED YOU

1971

Tabor College
Christ-centered education

400 South Jefferson
Hillsboro, Kansas 67063

HOWARD CLAASSEN, Ph. D.
Wheaton, Illinois

Topic "Science, Friend or Foe"

G. W. PETERS, Ph. D.
Dallas, Texas

RECIPIENTS OF
ALUMNI
MERIT AWARDS

P. E. SCHELLENBERG, Ph. D.
Bluffton, Ohio

ROGER WOLLMAN, LL. M.
Aberdeen, South Dakota

VIOLA WIEBE, B. A.
Hillsboro, Kansas

Topic "Tonic for Welt Smerz"

Epilogue

Most of the missionaries who worked in India under the organization of the Mennonite Brethren Church of North America came out of the prairie provinces of Central Canada or from the open wheat and corn growing regions of the Midwest in the United States. They came from small town and farm backgrounds, sent by their home churches to preach the gospel of their Christ. They came as white men and women during the period of the British Raj. They came with the understanding that somehow or other the cultural, social, political and technological patterns with which they were familiar in their home countries characterized the waves of the future, that patterns such as those common in India were bound to be replaced. They came with teachings of social equality. They came from countries in which answers to questions about social order were almost always given in terms of "integration," "melting pots" and "consensus," almost never in terms of the compartmentalization of social differences. They came as critics of what they considered the superstitions and false beliefs of the people they met. They came with a "new wine" they believed could never be fully contained within the caste and other structures of Hindu civilization.

The Mahbubnagar area to which the Mennonite missionaries came was drought prone and very poor.* It was an area in which laborers, particularly laborers at the lowest social levels, frequently found it difficult to earn livings, an area in which certain groups were less well tied than other groups into local rounds of life.

The overwhelming majority of the people in the Mahbubnagar region had always lived in villages. Social patterns here were thoroughly interrelated with regional patterns and the time-honored patterns of Indian Civilization. Families were linked into castes and caste-like units. The rights and responsibilities of an individual as a member of a caste were correlated with this unit's position in the hierarchically ordered caste system. Whereas the missionaries came emphasizing the importance of faith and belief, the villagers of the Mahbubnagar region were involved in a system which was itself defined as sacred, a system in which the performance of one's duties as these were socially defined was considered important in this life as well as in all future lives, whatever one's beliefs might be.

The reflective traditions of Hinduism were certainly evident in the villages of the area. But more important by far in the daily lives of the villagers were local traditions in belief and practice. The Nizam's state of Hyderabad (now largely a part of Andhara Pradesh) was a Muslim state, and Muslims dominated political life and the trade and service sectors of the economy. Most people were illiterate. Few traveled far. The most frequently approached deities were the favored deities of particular villages, the deities that protected villages, the deities associated with particular illnesses and the deities able to grant particular favors. The names of people associated them with one or another deity and were usually given in consideration of factors such as order of birth, conditions of birth and astrological signs. Many religious practices had to do with the accumulation of favor and the avoidance of disfavor among the deities important in daily life. The people used potions and mantras in protecting themselves from evil. They wore amulets, assuring support more effective than the supports they could assure for themselves. They knew that the covetous eye of another could be warded off with *disti bomas* (protection-giving images). They knew that leather

---

*My book, *Christians in India: The Mennonites of Mahbubnagar* (19 Millers Road, Bangalore: Christian Institute for the Study of Religion and Society, 1988) is a thorough sociological analysis of the entire Mennonite Brethren mission program in the Mahbubnagar area, and its outcomes.

could be used to scare away certain devils, that the spirits of those who had died unnaturally could return to hinder or help former acquaintances and relatives in the redress of grievances. They knew that certain spirits and tendencies were to be avoided, others appeased or encouraged. They knew that it mattered how one prepared to travel, precisely when one began a new venture, arranged a marriage or named a child, and on which day of the week one traveled in a particular direction. They knew that certain practices could help ensure the safety and usefulness of their animals and that deities often wanted to be propitiated.

The Mennonite missionaries responded to the situation they found in the Mahbubnagar area by establishing mission compounds. This response was in part inherited from earlier missionaries. It was also in part mandated in the context. The Baptists, Methodists and others the missionaries encountered when they first arrived worked out of such stations, and the missionaries soon understood that differences mattered. Whatever their teachings of brotherhood, the styles of life they sought to maintain for reasons of health, effort and emotional stability were very different from the styles the majority of their converts could approach. The Untouchables at the very bottom of the social system (Gandhi called them *Harijans*, "Children of God"), the overwhelming majority of the converts to Christianity in the Mahbubnagar area, lived in little thatched huts and performed the most menial of services. The missionaries came out of contexts with very different understandings of cleanliness and susceptibility to illness, and saw their purposes more broadly than would have been possible had they associated themselves entirely with the majority of their converts.

Second, had they not understood when they first arrived, the missionaries soon came to understand that the stations provided a place of refuge both for themselves and their converts. Social and ownership patterns and conceptions of privacy in the villages had always been far more collectively defined than they were in the backgrounds of the missionaries. With their walls, caretakers and bungalows (usually two-storied), the mission compounds enabled the missionaries chances for study, reflection, language learning, family life, order and a kind of manageability that would not have been theirs otherwise. Many unsupported converts, meanwhile, needed support and a place to which to escape. As a missionary in the Mahbubnagar area once pointed out: "To become a Christian and live on in *some* of the villages meant a living death." It had to do with the possibility of being cut off from water and food supplies, earning opportunities and the chance to arrange marriages for one's children. It had to do with the possibility of complete social ostracism.

Third, the system of patronage between leaders and followers in a setting like rural Mahbubnagar's in the early years of the twentieth century encouraged the independent demonstration of power and recourse. And this proved possible out of the mission station setting. The missionaries had an access to power that enabled them to set up and conduct their programs without major opposition. Theirs were certain privileges under the colonial system and in the ties that often were possible with local *rajahs*.

Fourth, the Mahbubnagar setting was in many ways strange and difficult for the early missionaries. Many Europeans still wore "belts" for protection against cholera, and pith helmets for protection against the noonday sun, in the India of that day. Panthers, leopards, hyenas and deer could be found in the forests. Plague, smallpox, cholera and other diseases at times took on epidemic proportions, and famines periodically stalked the land.

Finally, ideologies of the time often encouraged the missionaries to believe that local institutions were in decay and that the patterns they were helping to introduce would someday sweep the land. The missionaries frequently referred to the local people as heathen or pagan, sometimes with all of the pejorative content such labelings could entail. Many of the social scientists of the day, with just as much of an ethnocentric orientation to the world, labeled the local people animists, superstitious, primitive, uncivilized, backward or underdeveloped, in acceptance of approaches then popular. Few Westerners of any description at the time failed to feel they had much more to offer than to learn. Their assumptions in general were that their own already industrialized countries had already achieved a level of development that other countries could only someday hope to achieve, and that progress in general meant development along the lines, or in relation to the stages, already accomplished by the "more developed" countries.

PAUL D. WIEBE has taught and done research as a sociologist out of Colleges and Universities in the United States, Malaysia, India and East Africa, under the auspices of agencies such as the American Institute of Indian Studies, The Centre for International Comparative Studies, Fulbright, the Ford Foundation and the Carnegie Corporation of New York. His books include **Social Life in an Indian Slum** (1975), **Indian Malaysians** (1978), **Tenants and Trustees** (1981), **Crisis in Uganda** (with Cole P. Dodge, 1985) and **Development Issues in Uganda** (with Cole P. Dodge, 1987). At present Dr. Wiebe is Principal of Kodaikanal International School, Kodaikanal, Tamilnadu.

5117 011

"**Sepia Prints, Memoirs of a Missionary in India,** is no ordinary report about missions. This personal chronicle offers the reader a rare opportunity to walk the roads of India through a crisp and descriptive writing style, enhanced by hundreds of photos. It is the testimonial of an international missionary family that has left its indelible footprints in India."

Wesley Prieb
Director of the Center for M.B. Studies
Tabor College, Hillsboro, Kansas

"**Sepia Prints** delightfully captures the development and challenges of a missionary project in India from 1903 through the early 1970s. It reads of a woman's deep involvement and dedication in a remarkable story made interesting with pictures and human interest incidents accumulated in chronological order spanning almost seventy years.

"Tomorrow's task is to inspire the next generation to sustain the progress and to become personally involved in improving the world. **Sepia Prints** gives us the background and provides the basis for creating a better standard for today's children, tomorrow's leaders."

James P. Grant
Executive Director of UNICEF

"I found myself stopping again and again to read extended passages. Your affection for India is evident throughout, and you have written a fascinating account of a family united in the service of its Church. **Sepia Prints** is truly a labor of love."

Nancy Landon Kassebaum
United States Senator

ISBN: 0-921788-03-7